BLACK FILMMAKERS

AFRICAN-AMERICAN ACHIEVERS

BLACK FILMMAKERS

Cookie Lommel

CHELSEA HOUSE PUBLISHERS
Philadelphia

Chelsea House Publishers

Editor in Chief Sally Cheney
Production Manager Pamela Loos
Art Director Sara Davis
Cover Designer Keith Trego

The Chelsea House World Wide Web address is
http://www.chelseahouse.com

**Produced by Pre-Press Company, Inc.,
East Bridgewater, MA 02333**

First Printing
1 3 5 7 9 8 6 4 2

Library of Congress Cataloging-in-Publication Data

Lommel, Cookie.
Black filmakers / Cookie Lommel.
p. cm. — (African-Americans achievers)
Includes bibliographical references.
ISBN 0-7910-5816-6 (alk. paper) — ISBN 0-7910-5817-4
(pbk.: alk. paper)
1. Afro-Americans in motion pictures. 2. Afro-Americans in
the motion picture industry. 3. Afro-American motion picture producers and directors—Biography. I. Title. II. Series.
PN1995.9.N4 L66 2001
791.43'089'96073—dc21   00-052333

Frontispiece: One of the leaders of a new age of black film-making, Spike Lee, on the set of his landmark film, Do the Right Thing.

CONTENTS

AFRICAN-AMERICAN ACHIEVERS

BLACK FILMMAKERS

1

The Birth of Race Movies

FILMMAKING IS A fairly recent invention, little more than a 100 years old. Compared with the long history of books, newspapers, and live theater, filmmaking is a very young form of entertainment. The history of filmmaking began in the 1880s, when experiments that manipulated moving photographs culminated in short productions. Popular culture was awestruck by the moving images first produced by photographer Eadweard Muybridge and then refined by inventors George Eastman and Thomas Edison, who patented a motion picture camera in 1888.

By the turn of the 20th century, Thomas Edison was projecting moving pictures that could be watched by a single viewer at a time on a *Kinetoscope*. His productions were simply slices of real life: people dancing, people working, and other unscripted images. These early moving pictures included blacks going about the business of their lives, and they may be considered the first genuine depiction of the black experience in the American movie industry.

Moving pictures soon enthralled the nation as the most popular form of entertainment. People were eager to see their world chronicled on film. By 1908, there were 10 million viewers paying a nickel or a dime to go to the theater. Movies were called

Although modern filmmakers look back at The Birth of a Nation *as a technical marvel of early filmmaking, most agree that the themes depicted in the film are offensive. In this still from the film, the KKK, depicted as heroes, chase away a division of black Union soldiers.*

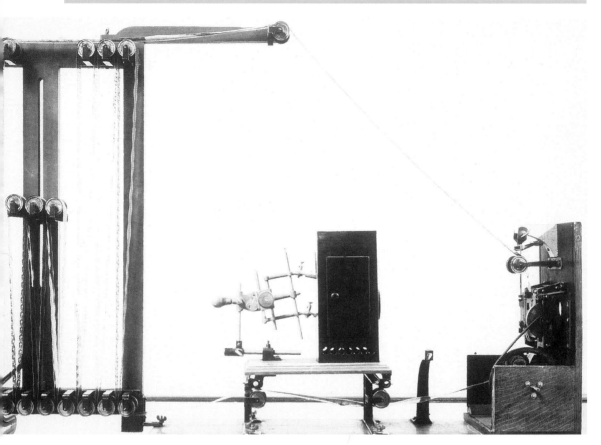

Thomas Edison's invention, the Kinetoscope, was the first machine that allowed for the viewing of motion pictures. The device revolutionized both communications and entertainment.

"the drama of the people," and financiers of the movie industry foresaw no end to their profits.

Initially, film subjects of African descent were represented as matter-of-factly as were Caucasians, although the filmed activities all took place in a segregated world—blacks living and working with blacks, and whites living and working with whites. But before too many years had passed, race was unmistakably brought to the audience's attention in unflattering and often insulting ways.

Initially, when Thomas Edison and other inventors designed the first motion picture cameras, it was not possible to edit the filmed images. But innovators like D. W. Griffith soon changed the nature of the staple short film offered to the movie-going public. Between 1908 and 1913, he and other filmmakers developed major techniques of filmmaking, including the use of alternating close-ups, medium shots, and panoramas; editing; mood-enhancing lighting; and narrative commentary. Newsreel footage and short films gave way to much longer movies with more complicated themes. It was now possible to persuade an audience to a point of view by using manipulated images. Acting, out of necessity, also became more professional.

Although the experience of African Americans with film, both as audience members and as filmmakers, began at the same point in history as it did for whites, two deliberately separate film traditions—one for blacks and one for whites—soon evolved. Slowly, white moviemakers of the newly developed Hollywood studio system began shaping their films to reinforce what they believed their audience wanted to see, and the image of blacks on film began to degrade, becoming little more than caricatures.

Blacks were relegated to roles of villains, cheats, and shiftless, subservient sidekicks. Between 1910 and 1911, for instance, moviegoers could see the slapstick, degrading antics of the clownish and uneducated black character Rastus. In movies like *How Rastus Got His Turkey*, *Rastus in Zululand*, *Rastus and Chicken*, and *Chicken Thief*, the audience was presented with a view of the black man (played by a white actor in blackface) stealing, flirting, lazing around, and failing to express himself in standard English. Another common black stereotype in early movies was the "Uncle Tom"—a virtuous black servant, endlessly loyal to his white master. In early movies black audiences would see characters who were nothing like themselves or members of their community.

A key element of all these early white-produced features was the contentment of the on-screen black characters with their lot. Open rebellion at social inequality simply did not exist on film. Filmgoers watching these features could assume that African Americans were satisfied with their place in a white-controlled society.

In the white-controlled fledgling movie industry, blacks were shut out from any part of the process of creating their image on film—white filmmakers controlled the cameras and white men wrote the scripts. White actors often assumed the roles of black characters by painting their faces black. As the industry attracted more financial backing, and the large Hollywood studios evolved, filmmakers took fewer and fewer risks, continuing to offer mostly stereotypical roles for blacks—material that was thought to appeal to white audiences and thus sell movies.

At first, control of the film industry, like control of nearly everything else, was in the hands of the dominant white culture. European immigrants like Carl Laemmle, Adolf Zukor, Samuel Goldwyn, Marcus Loew, Louis B. Mayer, and the Warner brothers quickly founded what would become the stronghouse studios of the 20th century. Their earliest studio efforts reflected what was seen as the will of the white majority in America.

Many African Americans were disturbed by how blacks were being portrayed in early films. They recognized what inventor Thomas Edison had predicted would come to pass as a result of motion picture technology: "Whoever controls the film industry controls the most powerful medium of influence over the public."

One of the first African-American filmmakers who worked to provide a positive image for blacks on film was William Foster, a vaudeville press agent. In 1910 Foster established the first black film company, the Will Foster Moving Picture Company, later renamed Foster Photoplay Company. His films were the first to show blacks in realistic situations, with realistic characters, not stereotypical ones. Foster produced three silent short movies, the first all-black films: *The Pullman Porter* (1910), *The Railroad Porter* (1912), and *The Fall Guy* (1913). However, Foster's films reached only a small audience, unlike those of many white film directors.

Soon after the release of Foster's films, white director D. W. Griffith demonstrated the potential political power of filmmaking. In 1915 he released a frighteningly racist epic called *The Birth of a Nation*. More than three hours long—longer than any film made up until that point—the silent film pulled out all the stops to convince its audience of the "real" history, at least according to Griffith, of the Civil War (1861–1865) and the Reconstruction Era (1865–1877). Griffith's film introduced many new filmmaking techniques— the use of night photography, outdoor backgrounds, total-screen close-ups, fade-outs, and panoramic shots—all of which delighted white audiences who saw the movie as a work of art.

Unfortunately, Griffith, the son of a Confederate soldier, had an agenda besides art to propagate: *The Birth of a Nation* presented negative images of blacks, while portraying members of the Ku Klux Klan, a southern group that often terrorized blacks, as heroic. In the film the black characters—usually white actors

Thomas Edison inspects a roll of film used for capturing motion pictures. The first movie cameras suffered from the absence of film editing, which was not introduced until a decade later.

in blackface—are lazy, violent, or subservient, and they are blamed for all the nation's social, political, and economic problems since the Civil War. One of the many controversial scenes of the film shows armed Klansmen on horses forcibly preventing blacks from voting.

When the silent film was released in February 1915, it was a box-office success. To celebrate the motion picture that justified the Klan's existence, members of the group burned a fiery cross on Stone Mountain in Georgia. The president of the United States at that time, Woodrow Wilson, endorsed the bigoted spectacle as well, supposedly exclaiming, "It's like writing history with lightning!"

D. W. Griffith's disturbingly racist film galvanized the African-American community, sparking intense protests in many cities. The National Association for the Advancement of Colored People (NAACP), an organization dedicated to obtaining rights for blacks, had already been concerned about the depiction of African Americans in film. The release of *The Birth of a Nation* moved the group to new activism. The NAACP tried to have the film banned, and it called for the first national black social protest and for citizens to boycott of the film. They were not alone in their outrage.

It was becoming increasingly clear that filmmaking—and the image of African Americans—was too important to leave in the complete control of white Hollywood film directors. In 1915, in reaction to the ugly stereotypes of blacks that were being perpetuated in popularly received films like *Birth of a Nation*, frustrated blacks formed the Independent African-American Filmmakers group. In 1918 the group, having received some financial backing from Universal Studios, answered *Birth of a Nation* with the release of its own *The Birth of a Race*.

The film was made by Emmett J. Scott, who had been the personal secretary of Booker T. Washington of the Tuskegee Institute, a well-regarded, historically black college. Although *The Birth of a Race* presented positive depictions of blacks, it had been

plagued by funding and production problems with Universal Studios. During the three years it took to film the story, distinctly African-American ideas ended up being replaced with supposedly universal ones. When it was finally released, the film drew little interest from black or white audiences.

But black filmmaking did not end there. *The Birth of a Race* was only a small part of an impressive alternative film tradition, a world of black moviemaking that would continue for the next three decades. Approximately 500 films, known as "race movies" would be made in the coming years, films with African-American producers and African-American actors. The need for new, positive ways to depict African Americans on film had spurred the development of a completely separate black filmmaking tradition.

From 1915 to 1925, the Independent African-American Filmmakers group financed its movies outside the power of the big-budget studios, in order to retain control of projects so that a black on film could be, "in his everyday life, a human being with human

Noble Johnson, seen standing to the far right in this publicity shot for the film Topsy and Eva, *started the Lincoln Motion Picture Company with his brother, George. The company was the first production studio owned and operated by African Americans.*

inclination and one of talent and intellect." But black filmmakers faced many obstacles. In Griffith's hands, filmmaking had begun to evolve as a skilled profession, and white control over the medium and its technology solidified; blacks were believed incapable of creating studio-quality films. In reality, African-American filmmakers had neither the resources nor the experience to produce movies that would satisfy their ever more sophisticated audiences.

However, pioneering black filmmakers would eventually rise to these challenges. Despite often low budgets, they figured out and then made use of the various techniques of filming and editing employed by big-name directors like D. W. Griffith.

Two such talented African-American filmmakers, actor Noble Johnson and his brother George Johnson, founded their own company in 1916. Named the Lincoln Motion Picture Company, the organization was the first movie company organized by African Americans to produce serious motion pictures for black audiences. Based in California, the Lincoln Company went on to produce an average of one film a year for the next six years—movies that portrayed blacks as educated, well-to-do professionals with comfortable, middle-class lifestyles. The Johnson pictures also had a professional look to them.

The company offered several films that broke the stereotypes persistent in white films of the day: *The Realization of a Negro's Ambition* in 1916 and *A Trooper of Troop K*, in 1917, and *By Right of Birth*, in 1921. *The Realization of A Negro's Ambition* featured a young engineer from Tuskegee Institute who saves the life of a white woman and goes on to succeed in her family's oil business. *A Trooper of Troop K* dramatized the massacre of black troops in the U.S. Army 10th Cavalry during its campaign against Mexican bandits and revolutionaries in 1916. *By Right of Birth* depicted successful middle-class black life, not clowns in blackface or hardened criminals.

Noble Johnson was not only president of this pioneering black studio but also one of the most handsome actors of the silent screen. An impressive looking performer who stood 6' 2" and weighed 215 pounds, Noble was a star of the silent era. He maintained a separate acting career as an established contract player at Universal, appearing in roles with some of Hollywood's biggest screen stars of the time, usually cast as an "exotic" Latino, Native-American, Egyptian, or of course black. Eventually his commitments to the Hollywood studio forced him to give up the presidency of the Lincoln Company, which dissolved in 1923 because of financial problems.

As black films became established as a separate tradition from that of white films, the average white audience remained racist, subscribing to the misrepresentations and clichés presented in popular Hollywood films. In films depicting black soldiers returning from serving their country in World War I (1914–1918), the men would not carry guns when they disembarked from their ships. Over the coming years a constant procession of black characters were portrayed as secretly wanting to be white or being prone to violence and rape. Filmmakers and studio heads clung to whatever stereotypes appealed to their white majority audience, perhaps fearing to alienate them with radical ideas about justice and equality.

Over the next five years, from 1915 to 1920, more than 30 companies like the Lincoln Motion Picture Company formed to produce race movies. By the 1920s several small silent-picture studios had sprung up across the nation in cities such as Chicago, Kansas City, Los Angeles, New York, and Philadelphia. Not all were owned by African Americans, but all the owners understood that the key to their box office success was the positive portrayal of the African American, an image denied at that point by mainstream Hollywood.

2

Enter the Midnight Ramble

B Y THE EARLY 1920s the motion picture rapidly became a potent force shaping 20th-century American culture. The impact on audiences of the larger-than-life movie screen pervaded every part of American life. Movies defined what was good and what was evil, what was right and what was wrong. They also shaped conventions of patriotism, romantic love, and even personal appearance. Moviegoers flocked to theaters to see idealized projections of their own aspirations and lives on the screen. But the silver screen depicted experiences not equally shared by all Americans. Who would want to identify with a servant, villain, or buffoon rather than a cowboy, queen, or war hero?

The discrimination between blacks and whites institutionalized on screen was simply a reflection of real life. Laws in many parts of the United States mandated the segregation of the races, preventing African Americans from mixing with whites. These segregationist "Jim Crow" standards had been signed into law by the U.S. Supreme Court in 1896, the same year that Edison introduced the large screen projector that made mass viewing of motion pictures possible. Because of segregation, blacks could attend

One of early filmmaking's most influential figures was Oscar Micheaux, shown here in the theatrical release poster from his film The Exile.

the theater only if they went to "colored" movie houses or to public movie houses only between midnight and 3:00 A.M. The low-budget, independent "race movies" were relegated to these showings, and thus came to be referred to as "the Midnight Ramble." Black films became a segregated, as well as separate, tradition.

When the movie business first started at the beginning of the 20th century, African Americans were leaving the South for the North in record numbers. They went to establish a better life than they could make in the South, which was cash poor and riddled with old hatreds. Most importantly, black teachers, doctors, and laborers went North to establish lifestyles parallel to those found in the dominant white society—to lead middle-class lives. The ordinary white citizen knew little of the everyday lives of blacks; stories that sensationalized rather than depicted the black experience were much more likely to attract their attention. Black Americans knew more about white Americans than whites had bothered to learn about blacks.

This situation was mirrored in popular culture. In Hollywood movies, blacks were ignored or trivialized. But the makers of race movies knew their audiences craved more, that they wanted to see movies peopled with a range of real characters that had some grounding in their own lives. Race movies addressed disturbing topics like lynchings, racial injustices, social issues like alcoholism and abuse, as well as color and class issues in the black community. In a segregated world, black audiences flocked to see the movies that had meaning for them.

Race movies got their start in Chicago, which in the early part of the 20th century was the home of many black and white silent movie studios. The city served both as a cultural center for African Americans and a lightning rod that attracted a vast amount of African-American talent—for example, the vaudeville performers who acted in silent films made by Foster Photoplay Company, which was based in Chicago. The city was also the birthplace of Ebony Films, a black-owned race movie studio run by Luther Pollard that produced slapstick comedies for black and white audiences.

In Chicago's sophisticated urban setting, blacks assumed a lifestyle of relative freedom, along with an income that allowed them to express themselves as they wanted. Members of the increasingly prosperous middle class had enough money to spend on movie tickets and enough self-esteem to dislike the prevailing Hollywood stereotypes, which continued to assault them in films, cartoons, and the press. African Americans turned to race movies for the chance to see characters and issues that applied to their world.

Oscar Micheaux began his career as a writer. When he wasn't allowed to direct a film version of his book, The Homesteader, *Micheaux decided to produce and direct the film himself.*

One black filmmaker who produced in Chicago and New York City would soon come to dominate the race movies industry during the first half of the 20th century. In 1918 Lincoln Motion Pictures had extended an offer to a black South Dakota homesteader named Oscar Devereaux Micheaux, the author of a series of well-received novels that were based on his experiences as a rancher. Micheaux was remarkably successful at promoting his books to his mostly white neighbors in South Dakota. The Lincoln Company wanted to option Micheaux's first book in the series, *The Homesteader*, which had been published in 1914.

Difficulties with the production deal developed. Micheaux demanded that he direct the filming of his book, although he had no directing experience. The deal fell through, but Micheaux was intrigued by the motion picture process. He decided to produce and direct *The Homesteader* himself. Released in 1919, it was the first of many more race movies that the newly formed Micheaux Film and Book Company would make. Micheaux films would range over a variety of topics and genres, from romance to comedy to drama to adventure, all with black men and women as their heroes.

Micheaux came to be known as a maverick, because he was the first black filmmaker to make feature-length films, also referred to as photoplays, and the first to make films that were controversial. Micheaux persisted with his goals in the face of tremendous obstacles, explaining in one interview, "One of the greatest tasks of my life is to teach that a colored man can become anything." He later noted his filmmaking philosophy had a distinct purpose: "I have always tried to make my photo plays present the truth, to lay before the race a cross section of its own life, to view the colored heart from close range."

Although Oscar Micheaux did not always direct or craft his actors' lines well, his vision was unflinching. He used all the drama and passion that the screen was able to project to say what he wanted. Micheaux took it upon himself to confront the social and cultural issues of his time.

And there was much civil unrest in the United States during the latter part of the decade. In Chicago, the summer of 1919 came to be called "Red Summer" because of the intensity of racial tensions resulting as white veterans returning from World War I competed with blacks for factory jobs in the city. Riots ensued, and blacks fought back with unusual ferocity in the face of racism. Micheaux was accused of fanning the flames with his controversial films, but his films continued to find a supportive black audience, and he continued to make them.

Before the Red Summer riots, Oscar Micheaux had already produced a stinging response to racial violence in his film *Within Our Gates* (1919). Based on the story of the Southern lynching of a black man named Leo Frank, the film was the first movie to show racial intimidation, lynching, and rape from the African-American point of view. *Within Our Gates* was so controversial, it was withdrawn from circulation almost immediately after its release.

In the more than 30 films that he made, Micheaux tackled an amazing variety of topics, and managed to keep his book and film business a healthy concern for more than 30 years. He did so by retaining an astonishing level of control over his material. Micheaux booked his own screening dates on the road, financed and produced his own films, recruited his own actors, made and distributed all of his own films, stuck to a tight production schedule and budget, and made the critical transition from silent movies to "talkies"—motion pictures with sound—at the right time.

In fact, Oscar Micheaux was the only black producer to successfully make the transition to the prohibitively expensive "talkies," which were introduced in 1927 with the first feature sound movie, *The Jazz Singer*. When sound movies replaced the silent films, black filmmaking changed dramatically and modern technology ushered in a new era of the midnight ramble, as race movies continued to be called. Although the costs involved in making sound movies almost bankrupted Micheaux, he managed to survive while other filmmakers went under.

The solid market for race movies encouraged filmmakers and independent production companies to make more and more films for blacks. A survey taken in 1929 revealed that 461 theaters catered exclusively to black audiences, all providing showcases for Micheaux's race movies and those of other black filmmakers. Most of these all-black theaters were located in the South and Southwest, although some were found in the North as well. A few, like the Walker

Palace, built in Indianapolis, Indiana, were owned and run by black entrepreneurs, and provided luxury accommodations such as boxed theater seats. Although race movies themselves were often underfinanced and all black filmmakers had to cut corners while making them, audiences still loved them despite the crudeness of some of the products.

In 1929, the stock market crash that precipitated the nation's economic woes in the Great Depression reduced theater attendance to an all-time low. But Micheaux was a legendary penny-pincher, a trait that served him well during those hard times. The owner of the Apollo Theater in the New York City borough of Harlem agreed to finance him, knowing Micheaux would be a good investment.

Throughout his career, Micheaux occasioned controversy, both from whites who did not approve of the independent black film industry and from blacks who objected to some of the troublesome plots of his films. In the silent film *Body and Soul* (1925), actor Paul Robeson portrays a con man masquerading as a preacher who betrays the trust of his congregation. Speculators believe that a showing of *The Exile* (1931) was stopped because of a controversial scene that depicted a black man's romantic involvement with a woman who could "pass"—that is, she appears to be white. Often Micheaux's controversial films simply showed the harsh realities and the burdens of a black community unacknowledged by a fearful public. These issues were given voice in *God's Step Children* (1938), a story of racial class and skin color. The film disturbed some audiences so much that they walked out during a scene where a white man knocks down a black girl and spits on her. Micheaux defended his choice of themes for his movies time and again. Theaters would occasionally refuse to show his most controversial works, or would stop their airing part way through.

Micheaux himself answered his critics with courage and a sophisticated understanding of the

OD'S STEP CHILDREN

An example of a lobby card, or advertisement, for God's Step Children distributed in theaters. Although completing the movie was difficult, the final product gave audiences an unswerving look at racial tensions in America.

search for truth. In an article he wrote for the *Philadelphia Afro-American*, he said, "My results might have been narrow at times . . . but in those limited situations, the truth was the predominant characteristic. It is only by presenting those portions of the race portrayed in my pictures in the light and background of their true state, that we can raise our people to greater heights."

Not all of Micheaux's obstacles were philosophical. Black filmmakers contended with the problem of less financing and less technical experience than was available to their Hollywood counterparts. Yet ingenuity often provided an answer to troublesome production concerns. *God's Step Children*, for example, was mostly shot in a friend's home because its stairwell had good lighting conditions.

Micheaux studied the work of other actors and filmmakers constantly, in order to incorporate their techniques into his own work. He wanted his films to have the professional qualities as those found in Hollywood films, even though his movies were not made with the same budget. He was a strong and driven man, and his concern for his business was unequaled. He controlled every aspect of his movie production—

King Vidor, a white director, released the musical Hallelujah, *which included an all-black cast. Vidor's film is an example of Hollywood's pursuit to create films—particularly musicals—that appealed to both black and white audiences.*

bicycling his prints from theater to theater; haggling for rental fees; and serving as director, producer, editor, promoter, and sometimes even cameraman. He managed to get movies made every year with remarkably low budgets, and was successful when others were not.

To keep costs down, Micheaux ran his company as a family affair. His brother Swan Emerson Micheaux served in several different capacities—as business manager, secretary, treasurer, and general booking manager. Oscar's wife, actress Alice Russell, whom he married in 1920, appeared in several of his films. The couple maintained a home in Montclair, New Jersey, but their business kept them on the road. When Swan decided to leave the company, Alice took charge of the office.

Hollywood realized that there was money to be made in black films. Tinseltown began to tap into the race movie market, particularly after the development of sound movies. During the 1930s and 1940s, mainstream Hollywood produced black-cast musicals and films produced especially for black audiences.

Hallelujah (1929), for example, was a King Vidor-directed black musical under white control that played very successfully in black theater houses. The film showcased the musical talents of black artists, as it soon became apparent that the key to success in Hollywood "crossover" movies—films that appealed to blacks and whites—was a lot of singing and dancing. As the motion picture industry continued to grow, the business became financially successful for many studios. By 1940, there were about 400 black theaters in America and 15,000 reserved for whites.

But during this same time, the quality of race movies—films addressing the characters and issues that black audiences wanted to see—began to deteriorate. Forced to adapt to a shrinking share of the market, Oscar Micheaux began to make different kinds of films, with less social content. White producers began to dominate in the race movie market, and by 1948 the era of independent black filmmakers was over. That was the year that Oscar Micheaux released his last film, *The Betrayal*. Promoted as the "Greatest Negro photoplay of all time," it opened in downtown New York at a white theater, where it attracted major attention, but did not do well financially.

Oscar Micheaux died in 1951 in relative obscurity. Throughout the course of his long career, he had written, directed, and produced 35 feature-length pictures, creating work that represents the core of early African-American cinema. Because of his work, Micheaux had a lasting influence on black film tradition up until the modern-day era. His mark on the profession was so profound that in 1986 the Directors Guild of America (DGA) recognized him with an honorary membership. After his death, however, no other black film directors took his place for many years.

Ironically, Micheaux's greatest contribution to filmmaking is often viewed by contemporary black audiences as his greatest shortcoming: some film historians cannot forgive Micheaux's focus on the interests and outlooks of the black bourgeoisie. His films never centered on the ghetto, and seldom dealt with despair. Instead they concentrated on the problems of passing for white or the difficulties facing "professional people."

To appreciate Micheaux's films one must understand that he was moving as far away as possible from the Hollywood studio's version of African Americans, with its prevalence of blacks as jesters and servants. He wanted to give his audience something "to further the race, not hinder it." Ultimately, his films were the direct opposite of the popular films—the products of the Hollywood studio system—that were shaping the image of African Americans throughout the 1930s and 1940s.

3

Mainstream Hollywood

By THE 1930S, most major motion picture studios were based in Hollywood, California, and were under the control of white European immigrants. Just as had happened in the early 1900s, the films produced in the 1930s contained parts for African Americans that appealed to a white audience, not a black one. The roles were typically stereotypes—black male actors portrayed Uncle Toms or singing, dancing buffoons. Both black men and women played domestic servants, usually in comical roles in which they were required to speak with a black dialect and in Southern slang.

These Hollywood films, which were being produced during a time of an immense economic downturn known as the Great Depression, boasted the highest number of black actors carrying mops and pails or lifting pots and pans than in any other period in motion picture history. The servants were always ready and willing to assist the boss, and always ready to lend a helping hand when times got hard.

Although the roles may have been demeaning, they were nonetheless paid professional jobs for working actors. In that aspect, the 1930s were a prosperous age for individual black performers. The bona fide

An image of Lena Horne dominates the theatrical release poster for the film Cabin in the Sky. *Horne, one of the first black performers to be signed to a multi-year contract by a Hollywood studio, was often used for singing and dancing performances in predominantly white films.*

JAMES CRUZE
presents

BIG
BOY **GUINN
WILLIAMS**

AND THAT SHUFFLIN' LAUGH-MAKER

STEPIN FETCHIT

IN

"*the BIG FIGHT*"

with
LOLA LANE
and
RALPH INCE

Distributed by ATLANTIC PICTURES CORPORATION

Despite his stereotypical performances as a slow-witted, shuffling character, Stepin Fetchit was one of the first black actors to receive top billing for the films he appeared in. His importance in promoting films can be seen in this theatrical poster for the film The Big Fight.

star was Stepin Fetchit, a vaudeville veteran whose roles were the first to mark the transition of African Americans in white films from field clown to house handyman. As a result, Fetchit became the era's first distinctive black film personality, although he played slow, dim-witted, and foot-shuffling characters. Fetchit appeared in more than 26 films from 1929 to 1935. Indeed, he was the first African-American man to receive featured billing in major Hollywood movies, including the 1929 black-cast musical *Hearts in Dixie*.

Fetchit's films are seldom shown today, and if they are, his scenes are usually edited out to avoid offending African Americans. Still, his place in film history remains significant. For his pioneering contributions, Fetchit received a special Image Award from the NAACP in 1976 and was elected to the Black Filmmakers Hall of Fame in 1978. When Stepin Fetchit successfully broke down doors that had been previously closed to black actors, he made it possible for thousands of others to walk through.

Of all the black servants in the Shirley Temple films of the 1930s and 1940s, none was more closely associated with her than tap dancer Bill "Bojangles" Robinson, who costarred with her in no fewer than four features. In their biggest hit together, *The Littlest*

Rebel, Robinson played her guardian, marking perhaps the first time that a black servant was made responsible for a white life on film. Although labeled an Uncle Tom by some critics because he played the familiar compliant servant role, Robinson, unlike Fetchit, was articulate and consistently reliable. His dependability and air of sophistication perhaps explains why there were seldom complaints about Bill Robinson's performances as there were against Fetchit's.

Meanwhile, it took an English studio to display the talents of Paul Robeson, a well-known black actor and star of race movies, who did not fit as easily into one of Hollywood's subservient roles. In 1933 he starred in the British production of *Emperor Jones*, the first film to star a black actor with a white supporting cast. In the film, Robeson plays a railroad porter who escapes from a chain gang and later becomes king of a Caribbean nation. However, the motion picture was an exception to most of the kinds of films being produced at the time.

Black actresses also received a share of stereotypical roles in the 1930s, playing the maids or nannies who were confidantes, playmates, and important plot fixtures. The domestic servants in 1930s films were almost always overweight and middle-aged, made up as jolly "Aunt Jemima" look-a-likes, wearing patchwork dresses and colorful head kerchiefs. Their stout black figures served as the perfect foils to their white mistresses, who ranged from child star Shirley Temple to sex symbol Mae West.

The black servant role reached a new height with the appearance of the first important "black film" of the 1930s, *Imitation of Life*. Based on Fannie Hurst's best-selling novel about a white woman and a black woman and their daughters, the film was released in 1934 by Universal Pictures at a time when a new social consciousness had infiltrated the motion picture industry. Already, President Franklin D. Roosevelt's election, the New Deal, the growing liberalism of the country, and the Depression itself had brought to American films a new world view and a new social

Although early in her career Louise Beavers was only offered roles in films as a maid or servant, as she appears here in Rainbow on the River, *her career developed and more challenging roles such as those in* Imitation of Life *and* The Jackie Robinson Story *were offered to her.*

order whereby many of the old racial prejudices were starting to be abandoned. *Imitation of Life* was an outgrowth of this new spirit. It prided itself on its portrait of the modern black woman, still a servant but now portrayed with dignity and character. *Imitation of Life* was directed by John Stahl and starred an integrated cast, including the black actress Louise Beavers.

Beavers had appeared in a number of maid roles before *Imitation of Life*, starring opposite such Depression heroines as Jean Harlow and Mae West. She had made her film debut as a cook in the 1927 film *Uncle Tom's Cabin*, but her greatest part was that of the reluctant entrepreneur and heartsick mother in *Imitation of Life*, in which she costarred with the white actress Claudette Colbert. She won substantial critical acclaim for her performance as a black mother whose light-skinned daughter rejects her in an attempt to pass as white.

When the "enlightened" post–World War II spirit virtually obliterated the servant figures, Louise

Beavers shifted gears as well to play Jackie Robinson's mother in the 1950 film *The Jackie Robinson Story*. She went on to perform in several films until her final appearance in 1960 in the television series *The Facts of Life*, in which she played the maid Beulah. That role had been performed first on the radio by Hattie McDaniel, another prominent black actress of the era.

Like Beavers, McDaniel was also known for her roles as a black maid or obedient servant, but she often brought to them a "take-no-mess" attitude. Audiences of the 1930s responded to her excessive showmanship, her brashness, and her audacity. The opposite of Louise Beavers, McDaniel became the one servant of the era to speak her mind fully, a spirit echoed in many of her films of the 1930s. Her most famous role was that of Mammy, the O'Hara family's faithful servant in the Civil War epic *Gone with the Wind*. For that performance, McDaniel received an Oscar for Best Supporting Actress in 1938, becoming the first African American to win an Academy Award.

Hattie McDaniel brought a new approach to the typical servant role that many black actors and actresses were confined to. Her outspoken, no-nonsense performance in Gone with the Wind *won her an Academy Award for best supporting actress in 1938.*

HOLLYWOOD PRODUCTIONS *Presents*

Herbert JEFFREY

AND HIS HORSE "STARDUSK" *in*

HARLEM RIDES the RANGE

WITH

Spencer **WILLIAMS**   *Clarence* **BROOKS**

F.E. MILLER • ARTIE YOUNG • LUCIUS BROOKS
TOM SOUTHERN • JOHN THOMAS • WADE DUMAS
LEONARD CHRISTMAS *and* **THE FOUR TONES**

Story by SPENCER WILLIAMS *and* F.E. MILLER
A RICHARD C. KAHN PRODUCTION

Distributed by
SACK AMUSEMENT ENTERPRISES

ALL-COLORED CAST

Spencer Williams made a name for himself with roles in black westerns such as Harlem Rides the Range, *of which a poster is shown here. He later directed several films during the 1940s.*

In an effort to provide better, more sophisticated roles for blacks in the entertainment industry, an agreement was made in the spring of 1942 between Hollywood studio heads; Walter White, the executive secretary of the NAACP; and Wendell Willkie, the defeated Republican presidential candidate in 1940. When White and Willkie held a luncheon discussion with film producer Daryl Zanuck, he acknowledged that although he was responsible for one-sixth of the pictures made in Hollywood at the time, the problem of black stereotyping had never occurred to him. In the future, he and several other producers pledged, they would give fair, reasonable treatment of blacks in their movies.

Although the servant era was finally facing its demise, the plight of black performers did not improve very much during the following decades. From the late 1940s through the early 1960s, Hollywood studios, acknowledging the growing African-American market, produced films that would appeal to black audiences. But with the exception of several 1940s films directed by the actor Spencer Williams, Hollywood suffered from a severe shortage of black-directed films. Spencer had previously starred in Hollywood black Western films such as the *Bronze Buckaroo* (1938) and in *Harlem Rides the Range* (1939), along with black actor Herbert "the Singing Cowboy" Jeffrey. During the 1940s Spencer wrote, starred in, and produced eleven films ranging in themes from religious, as in *Blood of Jesus* (1941), to dance, as in *Beale Street Mama* (1947).

During the 1940s the role of blacks in Hollywood films eventually shifted from domestic servant to entertainer. By that time many African-American singers and dancers had achieved fame performing at nightclubs or jazz venues, and film provided them with yet another showcase. However, a special Hollywood-derived method evolved in which these entertainers were displayed on film without being included in the regular plot of the movie. Instead, Hollywood producers introduced specific musical interludes during which a black entertainer would perform, unimpeded by any story line. Frequently, the movie would include a nightclub scene so that the African-American star would appear in a "natural" setting.

Throughout the 1940s and 1950s, this format became so successful that there was hardly a film made in which there was not at least one performance by a black entertainer. One performer seriously affected by this built-in cutting procedure was the singer Lena Horne. Perhaps the biggest African-American attraction of the 1940s, Horne had appeared at Harlem's Cotton Club nightclub at age 16, sung at many of New York's popular nightclubs, and successfully performed on Broadway with Lew Leslie's *Blackbirds of 1939*. NAACP executive secretary Walter White had taken a personal interest in her career, convinced she could help alter the image of blacks in American movies.

In her early films, Horne appeared as herself. Always elegantly dressed, she performed her musical number, and then disappeared. In her first Hollywood

Lena Horne was often discouraged by the limited roles she was given in films. It wasn't until the release of Cabin in the Sky, *of which a still is shown here, that Horne was better able to display her talent as an actress.*

motion picture, the 1942 film *Panama Hattie*, from Metro-Goldwyn-Mayer (MGM), Horne's only scene was a musical number in which she belted out a Latin song, danced with the Berry Brothers, and then exited. While her brief appearance spawned letters from whites asking who the new "Latin American" discovery was, MGM was also accused by some angry blacks of attempting to pass her off as white.

The actress later described the limited role in her next film, *Thousands Cheer* (1943), as that of "a butterfly pinned to a column singing away in Movieland." Later in 1943 Horne went on to star in one of the biggest musicals of the decade, MGM's *Cabin in the Sky*. The script had sat on the MGM shelf for years due to concerns about whether an all-black production could make money. After producer Arthur Freed finally got the green light to make the film, it became the first musical with an all-black cast in nearly 14 years. The cast included many musical greats, including Louis Armstrong, Ethel Waters, and Duke Ellington.

Other all-black musicals followed. Also released in 1943 was *Stormy Weather*, which starred Lena Horne, and featured dancer Bill "Bojangles" Robinson and blues and jazz performers Cab Calloway and Fats Waller. *Ebony Parade* (1947) starred Dorothy Dandridge, Count Basie, Cab Calloway, and the Mills Brothers. These films of the 1940s attracted big-name talents that black audiences wanted to see.

By the 1950s, many social and political changes were affecting the motion picture industry. Because of blacklisting—the government's singling out of actors deemed sympathetic toward Communism—the industry lost some of its best talents. At the same time, box-office attendance had begun to drop as television sets entered homes across the nation. To attract people back to the theaters, the film industry began to explore more serious subjects.

The magical, romanticized, daydream quality of the old 1940s movies and musicals gave way to independent films infused with social messages, including explorations into the issues surrounding the integration of blacks into white society. With the gains made in the late 1940s, the subsequent decade provided an environment for the emergence of distinct black personalities who breathed new life into the roles of the black leading man. One of these personalities was Sidney Poitier.

Film historians have analyzed why Poitier was able to succeed at becoming a major star in mainstream American motion pictures at a time when other black actors could not even obtain roles. They observe that in the majority of his films, Poitier played a character who is an intelligent, educated man who speaks proper English, dresses conservatively, and has the best of table manners. The characters he played never acted impulsively or threatened the social system. For the white mass audience, Poitier was a black man who met their standards.

Poitier was also acceptable to the 1950s black audience as the epitome of black middle-class values and virtues. During the 1950s, as blacks gradually increased their political power, Poitier became a standard to live up to. He was the complete opposite of the shuffling, bowed-head, mumbling black characters of the previous decades. Both black and white Americans accepted Poitier, even though some blacks attributed this success to his mild-mannered, complacent roles, in which he often turned the other cheek whenever insulted or badgered.

In his first film, *No Way Out* (1950), Poitier introduced audiences to all of the characteristics that would come to define the actor's roles for the rest of the decade. Poitier played Luther Brooks, a young black doctor who tends to two white hoodlums wounded during an attempted robbery. When one of the men dies, the other then accuses Brooks of murder. Thereafter the young doctor is embroiled in controversy as he fights to prove his innocence. *No Way Out* to some degree captured the mood of postwar America and

A still of Sidney Poitier and Tony Curtis from the film The Defiant Ones. *Poitier received some backlash from the black community for appearing in roles where, although he was middle class and educated, he was still subservient to other white characters.*

painted an honest picture of its repressed racial hostilities. The film garnered critical praise, with the *New York Times* calling it "a harsh, outspoken picture with implications that will keep you thinking about it long after leaving the theater." But it failed to win a large audience.

Poitier later made a vivid impression in later roles: as a rebellious student in *The Blackboard Jungle* (1955), as a good-hearted dockworker in *Edge of the City* (1957), and as the lead opposite Dorothy Dandridge in George Gershwin's folk opera *Porgy and Bess* (1959).

Poitier's most important film of the decade was *The Defiant Ones* (1957), in which he starred as an escaped black convict handcuffed to a white prisoner, played by Tony Curtis, as the two escape from the law. Neither man likes the other, but by the movie's end, a deep bond has developed between them. After they are unchained, Poitier comes to the rescue of Curtis, not out of necessity but out of brotherly love. This film alienated a certain segment of the black audience. In some theaters, Poitier's character was showered with boos when he saved Curtis. For the first time, black audiences began to respond negatively to Poitier's self-sacrificing character. But to Poitier's credit, his tremendous acting ability almost demanded that the role and the film be taken seriously. Ironically, the role earned him an Oscar nomination for Best Actor. With that film he became Hollywood's first black leading man—and star.

During the 1950s, the tragic themes of "mixed race" and passing for white occurred in several important films, with the genre kicked off by the 1949 film *Lost Boundaries*, based on the *Reader's Digest* true story of a black New England family that passed as white for 20 years. The film tells the story of Scott Carter, a light-skinned black doctor unable to find employment because of segregation. At black hospitals he is rejected because he looks too white, and at white hospitals he is rejected for admitting that he is black. Finally, he moves with his light-skinned wife to a New England community where they keep their racial identity from their neighbors. They participate in community activities and function as a white family for years, until his enlistment in the U.S. Navy unearths his true identity.

Other films dealing with this theme followed. By far, the 1950's greatest biracial heroine was Sara Jane in Douglas Sirk's 1959 film *Imitation of Life*, a remake of the 1934 motion picture starring Claudette Colbert and Louise Beavers. The film focused on two issues that were much in the public's collective mind: race and emerging feminism.

In the 1959 version of *Imitation of Life*, Lana Turner plays a white single mother aspiring to be a famous actress. Her daughter, played by Sandra Dee, is the all-American sweetheart learning to grow up within a black and white family unit. She has a black nanny, played by Juanita Moore, who lives with and works for the family with her daughter, Sara Jane, played by Susan Kohner. The four women struggle to understand themselves and each other through various themes of social and personal conflict: male versus female, mother versus daughter, master versus servant, and most controversially, white versus black.

Sara Jane's mother chooses a life of acceptance and submission, accepting the notion that society is unchangeable and that the best thing a black person can hope for is a nice benefactress. Her light-skinned daughter, however, is not happy with her lot in life. Sara Jane denies her biracial background, hurts her mother's feelings, and runs away from home. Despite her flight, she is continually punished, whether it is by an abusive boyfriend or children at school, and she is forced to accept that she will never be white.

Sirk's 1959 film managed to surpass Stahl's 1934 version in its portrayal of American race and class relations. But a significant difference between the two versions is the portrayal of Sara Jane. In Stahl's version, the role is played by biracial actress Fredi Washington, while in Sirk's version a white actress, Susan Kohner, portrays the troubled girl.

Tragic tales like *Imitation of Life* were considered women's films, a 1940s genre that had been on the decline and that no longer guaranteed box-office success. Yet, *Imitation of Life* did quite well financially, attracting white audiences with its novel twist on a familiar soap opera plot and providing black audiences with a rare emotional release.

As the 1950s progressed, white filmmakers had begun to confront racial issues and handle them in relatively honest terms. However, the story lines tended to include happy endings, for the most part, and if any black anger—such as that expressed in one of Poitier's emotional outbursts—popped up, its impact was lessened by the picture's conclusion, when all difficulties and problems were resolved.

But as the United States neared the end of the decade, the nation was approaching a time of social upheaval, a new period during which racism would be revealed as a pervasive element in American society. The next decade would mark a time in which the American black man would assert himself culturally and articulate the rage he had suppressed through the years. That great social and political change—and its impact on Hollywood films—would render obsolete much of the work of black stars and personalities of the 1950s and would usher in a totally new type of black film and even a new type of black star. Suddenly, the mainstream Hollywood industry realized it could capitalize on this change in racial awareness.

4

Cinematic Diversity

THE 1960S MARKED an era of sit-ins, boycotts, marches, riots, and demonstrations that formed the transition from black cultural and academic integration to an African-American separateness and new cultural identity. The films of the period reflected this movement.

The first steps in the evolution of a new black film began with the appearance of black scriptwriters, providing films with realistic dialogue and characters. In 1960, black screenwriters were a rarity in Hollywood, but black playwright Louis Peterson had found some success with his adaptation for film of his successful off-Broadway play *Take a Giant Step*, the story of a young black man growing up in a white middle-class neighborhood.

Another black playwright, Lorraine Hansberry, had her play *A Raisin in the Sun* adapted to film in 1961. The story captured the tension of blacks enduring lives of violent desperation, a topic never dealt with before in the movies. Hansberry's tale took the audience into the hopelessness of the ghetto, revealing the matriarchal set-up in many black homes and examining how a hostile white society weakened the black male figurehead.

Raisin in the Sun, *based on the Lorraine Hansberry play, was one of the first films to present an accurate depiction of life in the ghettos and the challenges facing the black families who lived there.*

Set in a tiny southside Chicago apartment, *A Raisin in the Sun* follows the story of the Younger family. For years, matriarch Lena Younger has dreamed of getting out of the run-down flat she shares with her daughter, Beneatha, and son, Walter, and his wife and son. Lena's deliverance comes in the form of a $10,000 insurance policy left to her by her husband, which she uses to buy her dream house in the integrated suburbs. But in the wake of her dream, the personal problems of each member of the household clash with those of the others. As the restless, wayward son, Walter, Sidney Poitier gave one of his most critically acclaimed performances, heightened perhaps because his character differed so much from the established Poitier image. Black audiences could identify with his portrayal of a deeply troubled man.

Overall, the appeal of Sidney Poitier's integrationist roles became outdated as the 1960s progressed, and he began to receive harsh criticism. Dramatist Clifford Mason, writing in the *New York Times*, suggested that Poitier's Hollywood success was due to his ability to make whites comfortable. Black nationalist Larry Neal labeled Poitier "a million-dollar shoeshine boy" and "a good boy in a totally white world, with no woman to love or kiss, helping the white man solve the white man's problems." In the book *Framing Blackness: The African American Image in Film*, author Ed Guerrero noted that during this time "Poitier's 'ebony saint' image was wearing increasingly thin for black Americans; it did not speak to the aspirations or anger of the new black social consciousness that was emerging."

Even though Poitier's roles were of dignified men, the changing political attitudes in black America proved too much for him to continue making the same kind of films in the 1970s. The Academy of Motion Picture Arts and Sciences, however, did bestow on Poitier its highest honor for an actor in 1963. For his role of easygoing Homer Smith, an ex-

G.I. who helps a group of refugee nuns in the financially successful film *Lilies of the Field*, Poitier received an Academy Award, becoming the first black man to receive an Oscar for Best Actor.

After receiving his Oscar, Poitier went on to make more films that showed him as a savior to white characters. In *The Slender Thread* (1965), with Anne Bancroft, he becomes the black savior of a crazed white woman who has taken an overdose of pills. In *A Patch of Blue* (1966), he assists a poor, blind white girl. In *To Sir, with Love* (1967), he is a schoolteacher, oddly representative of the system that the old Poitier of *The Blackboard Jungle* had rebelled against.

Although Poitier was still the top black box-office draw in the country, his roles became out of place in the evolving separatist age of black versus white. Poitier's star faded after 1967, the year that three of his films made him Hollywood's premiere box-office draw. In *Guess Who's Coming to Dinner* he played the handsome suitor meeting his white fiancée's parents, Spencer Tracy and Katharine Hepburn; as a teacher in *To Sir with Love*, he wins the respect of his white, working-class students; and *In the Heat of the Night* he successfully investigates a murder as police detective Virgil Tibbs.

The theme of black families integrated into white neighborhoods, as reflected in *A Raisin in the Sun*, had strongly influenced white director Roger Corman, who in 1963 made a low-budget film entitled *The Intruder*. The film centered on a racist white man who drifts between small Southern towns inciting people to fight against court-ordered school desegregation. The racial animosities in the film result in bombings, burnings, and night rides of the KKK. Because he focused on the white-black integration theme that at the time was still a very taboo subject, Corman is to be commended for venturing to make such a film. Despite its melodramatic plot, *The Intruder* is historically important as part of American cinema's commitment to the civil rights movement.

Other white directors also addressed social issues of 1960s America during the first half of the decade. Four sensitive, low-budget films offered a realistic, yet cynical, look at black America and society.

John Cassavetes's *Shadows* (1961) was about a black girl who passes for white. Shirley Clarke's *The Cool World* (1963) follows the plight of 15-year-old Harlem native Duke and his gang, the Pythons. Clarke paints a realistic portrait of a Harlem neighborhood that would persuade Duke to believe a gun will give him power. While *Shadows* dealt with interracial romance and relationships on the screen, Sam Weston and Larry Peerce's *One Potato, Two Potato* (1964) was the industry's first portrayal of an actual interracial marriage. The film followed a custody battle between a divorced white husband and wife for their young daughter. When the former husband learns that his former wife has married a black man, he initiates a court battle to take the daughter away. These three films of the 1960s portrayed black protagonists demanding a chance to fulfill themselves on their own terms without having to live up to white standards. Behind their placid exteriors shone a glimmer of a great militant spirit.

That spirit is more apparent in the fourth film, *Nothing But a Man* (1965), the debut from writer-director Michael Roemer. The film was praised for its calm, dignified story about an average, everyday African-American railway laborer named Duff, who was played by Ivan Dixon. The film focuses on the relationship between Duff and his wife, as well as the realities of prejudice and racial distrust in their southern life.

The independent character of Duff, who refuses to defer to his racist white bosses, is a fitting precursor to the militant movement about to burst on the scene. Duff's quarrel is not only with his white oppressors but also with blacks who remain quiet in the face of oppression. The character would usher in a new style of black masculinity in the 1960s.

What remains the most intriguing aspect of the mid-to-late 1960s is the speed with which attitudes, outlooks, and opinions changed to reflect the new political consciousness. In dealing with racial situations, moviemakers had been accustomed to moving in cautious steps, in tune with the rhythm of the mass audience. During the 1960s, however, Hollywood appeared to lose track of the speed with which the mind of the mass audience was moving.

By 1966 Martin Luther King's philosophy of nonviolence had lost it hold in the minds of a new generation of black Americans. Before the end of the decade, Malcolm X had been assassinated, Stokely Carmichael had arrived with talk of black empowerment, and H. Rap Brown had made his famous statement, "Violence was as natural in America as apple pie." Riots had erupted in the Watts section of Los Angeles and in the cities of Cleveland, Detroit, Harlem, Philadelphia, and Washington, D.C. The president's National Advisory Commission reported that America was "moving toward two societies, one black and one white, separate and unequal." However, the Hollywood movies of the late 1960s would continue to reflect blacks in a complacent state of being. By the end of the decade, the motion picture industry would finally catch up and a new kind of black film would emerge.

The Learning Tree (1969) introduced the public to a new theme in film, a condemnation of the social system and the notion of separatism. But the film, which documents the life of a black child growing up in a racist town, became a historic motion picture for another reason. With this film, its director, Gordon Parks Sr., became the first black director of a major studio film. Finally, blacks were working behind the camera as well as in front of it.

Gordon Parks Sr. spent close to 20 years working as a photographer for Life *magazine before becoming the first black director of a major studio release with the film* The Learning Tree.

Parks was a multitalented author, photographer, and composer who had worked for about 20 years as a photographer for *Life* magazine. In 1963, he had received critical acclaim for his autobiographical novel *The Learning Tree,* and Warner Brothers had signed him to adapt the book for the screen. Gordon Parks not only directed but also wrote the screenplay and composed the score for the movie, which is an account of Parks's childhood in Cherokee Flats, Kansas, during the 1920s. Unlike other black characters of 1960s films, his race is not the major theme of the film. Parks's hero, played by Kyle Johnson, simply observes the world, learning from the harsh realities of racism and struggling to understand his relationships with friends and society in general.

The Learning Tree, based on the 1963 autobiographical novel of the same name by Gordon Parks, broke new ground in Hollywood. In the film Parks, who also wrote the screenplay and composed the score, details the harsh realities of racism in 1920s Kansas.

For the most part, the films produced during the late 1960s were used almost explicitly to make political statements. The new filmmakers wanted their products to reflect the changing times and to speak out on current social, political, and economic issues. In the decade to come, Sidney Poitier's films, with their interracial mass appeal, would find competition from a number of motion pictures that would reflect the new black consciousness emerging from the inner cities. These were films that dealt with issues rarely if ever seen on screen before—ghettos, prostitutes, hustlers, addicts, pimps and pushers, black despair, and rage. New filmmakers would begin to examine issues such as poverty, interracial marriages, and black survival within the narrow confines of the white world.

5

Heroes and Sheroes

IN THE EARLY 1970s two well-known African-American actors moved from on-screen roles to positions behind the camera with the purpose of making films for black audiences.

Renowned stage actor Ossie Davis, who had first appeared on-screen in *No Way Out* (1950), with Sidney Poitier and Ruby Dee, made his directorial debut with the 1970 United Artists action-comedy *Cotton Comes to Harlem*. Based upon the novel by African-American author Chester Himes, the fast-moving crime drama starred Godfrey Cambridge and Raymond St. Jacques as Harlem detectives Grave Digger Jones and Coffin Ed Johnson. The film was one of the first to capture the true atmosphere of Harlem, complete with shots of Seventh Avenue and 125th Street and other area landmarks such as the Apollo Theatre, the Spanish-American Barbershop, and Frank's Cafe. *Cotton Comes to Harlem* was a hit at the box office, and was subsequently followed by Davis's *Black Girl* (1972), *Gordon's War* (1973), and *Countdown at Kusini* (1976).

In 1972 Sidney Poitier made his directorial debut with *Buck and the Preacher*, a film in which he starred, along with his longtime friend Harry Belafonte.

During the 1970s a new genre of film, heavy on action and influenced by drugs and street justice, found its way into theaters across the country. Foxy Brown, starring Pam Grier, was a prime example of these "blaxploitation" films.

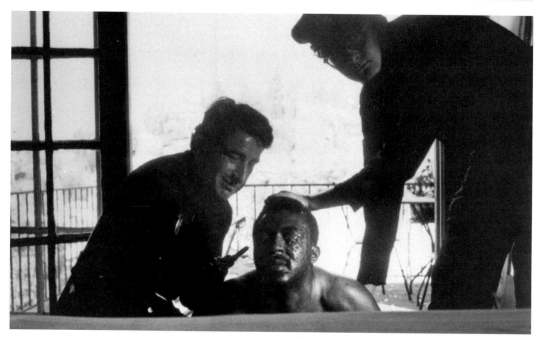

Melvin Van Peebles's 1971 film Sweet Sweetback's Baad Asssss Song, *a story of black street life, was the first commercially successful black-theme film to portray a black man coming out on top.*

The crossover Poitier of the 1960s sought to reconnect with the black audience with this tale about the period following the Civil War, when freed slaves were tracked down by bounty hunters and forced to return to unofficial slavery in the South. Poitier and Belafonte played freed slaves who outsmarted the bounty hunters.

As reflected in his 1980 autobiography, *This Life,* Poitier was aware of the alienation his own people felt from the characters he played during the late 1960s. After *Buck and the Preacher,* he continued directing films targeted directly at the black audience, including the 1973 romantic drama *A Warm December* and extremely popular all-black comedies in which he costarred with actor/comedian Bill Cosby—*Uptown Saturday Night* (1974), *Let's Do It Again* (1975), and *A Piece of the Action* (1977).

But other black filmmakers moved in an entirely different direction, creating a new kind of motion picture genre. The 1970s ushered in the era of "blaxploitation" films, named in later years for their gross exploitation of black stereotypes of crime, drugs, and guns. The movies all had a theme rooted in getting back at the white power structure and at authority figures. Between 1970 and 1980, major and independent movie studios released more than 200 films that featured major black characters and themes reflecting the African-American frustration with the status quo of race in America—and that featured strong male characters who were bad, tough, and in charge.

Many critics of 1970s blaxploitation films believed these movies pandered to the lowest of black so-called ghetto images, while borrowing heavily from mainstream Hollywood genres no longer used. There were black westerns, sci-fi fantasies, and horror movies. Blaxploitation even had its own kung fu flicks. But despite lackluster performances by the actors and shoestring budgets, the hip talk, sex appeal, and messages of black power made blaxploitation movies instant hits with black audiences.

Perhaps the first film hailed by critics as the absolute beginning of the blaxploitation era was Melvin Van Peebles's 1971 groundbreaking film *Sweet Sweetback's Baad Asssss Song*. It was the first commercially successful black-theme film that showed a black man coming out on top over the white establishment.

Van Peebles had made his feature-film debut while living in France, where he wrote, directed, and composed the music for *The Story of a Three Day Pass* (1967). The film's success helped him land a job directing the satirical comedy *Watermelon Man* (1970), starring Godfrey Cambridge. But *Sweet Sweetback's Baad Asssss Song*, which reveals black street life, cemented his reputation as a major African-American filmmaker.

Starring Melvin Van Peebles, who was also director, producer, and screenwriter, *Sweetback* vividly depicted the rejection of authority figures, with the black man triumphing over the white man. Van Peebles played Sweetback, a hustler on the run after he beats up white police officers while helping a young black revolutionary named Moo-Moo.

Melvin Van Peebles directed and starred in Sweet Sweetback's Baad Asssss Song, *a film, with its depiction of a black hero fighting against mostly white authority figures, that ushered in a new era of blaxploitation films.*

Sweetback manages to escape from the police as he works his way to the Mexican border. Several other black characters aid Sweetback in besting the white authority. A group of black children burn a police car and set him free the one time he is captured, and his intense sexuality persuades both black and white women to aid him in his escape.

Black film historian Thomas Cripps said of Van Peebles, "His startingly violent, truculent celebrations of black outlawry . . . lashed out at Hollywood classical conventions while drawing on an urban, youthful black and crossover audience." The film appealed to the inner-city youths because its contents included fighting, sexuality, and fleeing from the cops. The movie also broke a number of unspoken "race rules" of filmmaking. Police brutality was depicted as an everyday fact of life for black men, the inner cities were portrayed with unabashed honesty, and instead of the film ending with solutions the audience is left with questions about morality. The fact that a black man meets violence with violence and win despite a corrupt white system was a landmark theme in film. *Sweetback* offered a brand new image that Van Peebles would use to challenge black audiences.

The racial violence and sexual exploits depicted in *Sweetback* earned the film an X rating, but Van Peebles marketed the controversy as a reason to see the movie. Blacks flocked to the film, making it a commercial success. Perhaps an even bigger impact than the film itself was Van Peebles' ability to get his picture made as an independent filmmaker, outside of Hollywood's system, thus setting an example for future filmmakers.

If Van Peebles is the precursor to black-theme pictures infused with social statements, Gordon Parks's 1971 film, *Shaft*, simply underscored the new direction in film. *Shaft* ushered in yet another image of the black hero in blaxploitation films. The film starred Richard Roundtree as John Shaft, a respectable private detective who is hired to find a black gangster's daughter who has been kidnapped by the Mafia. John Shaft is laid-back yet self-assured, and most importantly, unintimidated by whites. He is the black man whom black communities have seen before, but never on-screen.

Shaft appealed to black and white audiences alike. It grossed $12 million in 1971, which single-handedly saved the studio that financed it, MGM, from financial ruin. The film's score composer, Isaac Hayes, earned an Academy Award for his work, and Parks went on to film the first sequel, *Shaft's Big Score!* in 1972.

One year after *Shaft*, Parks's son, Gordon Parks Jr., served as producer on what would become another important film of the blaxploitation era. *Superfly* starred Ron O'Neal as Youngblood Priest, a smooth cocaine dealer who runs the streets of Harlem. The controversial lead character created a dilemma for black audiences, who gave the film mixed reviews. Many blacks felt uneasy with the film's nonchalant portrayal of drug selling and use. However, *Superfly* tapped further into the new psyche of black youth in the inner city, and the fantasy of triumphing over authority.

Like *Sweetback*, the film *Superfly* underscored the theme of black outlaw as antihero. When all was said and done, black audiences identified with the simple tale of a man struggling to get out of the drug business and survive as an under-skilled, undereducated minority in a white man's world. Within two months of its release in 1972, the film made $1 million, and for a while out-grossed every other movie on the market.

"A lot of films today are about victims, but most of the films then were about empowerment," said Pam Grier, the blaxploitation era's undisputed leading lady in a 1996 *Entertainment Weekly* interview. Discovered while working as a switchboard operator for a movie studio, Grier quickly rose to blaxploitation fame in a series of films where she fought toe-to-toe with pushers, cops, and gangsters, all while keeping every hair in

Cooley High *was director Michael Schultz's second film. He began his directorial career with* Honeybaby, Honeybaby, *released in 1974.*

place. In fact, her sexuality was as much a part of her films as her ability to fight white and male oppression. In such black-action films as *Foxy Brown* (1972), *Sheba Baby* (1975) and her biggest hit, *Coffey* (1973), Grier gained immense popularity, selling out theaters in both black and white neighborhoods.

Tamara Dobson was the era's other female "shero." Starring in the film *Cleopatra Jones* (1973), Dobson was the blaxploitation era's female James Bond. In the title role, Dobson plays a "special agent" for the U.S. government who travels around the world to battle drug lords. Dressed in expensive furs, head wraps, and jewelry, Dobson is the picture of elegance while fighting crime. Dobson went on to star in the sequel, *Cleopatra Jones and the Casino of Gold* (1974), solidifying her place as one of the blaxploitation era's most important players.

Yet despite the presence of high-profile female leads such as Pam Grier and Tamara Dobson, the depiction of women in blaxploitation movies was at best stereotypical and oftentimes degrading. However, because of the "shero" qualities in the characters of Grier and Dobson, they also represented a step above the usual niche of females in blaxploitation films, who are simply present as love interests for the heroes.

The early 1970s were dominated by the blaxploitation theme of black antihero getting one over on "the man." The success of *Sweetback*, *Shaft*, and *Superfly* caught the attention of movie studios, which soon began to churn out similar fare. Suddenly, theaters were filled with blaxploitation films—gangster films such as *Black Caesar* (1973), action-revenge

thrillers like *Slaughter* (1972), horror films such as *Blacula* (1972) and *Scream Blacula Scream* (1973), and crime flicks like *Hit Man* (1972), *Cool Breeze* (1972), and *Detroit 9000* (1973).

Breaking away from the themes of blaxploitation films, Michael Schultz's Cooley High *painted an engrossing picture of black teen life in the 1960s.*

Although some black actors, directors, and writers were recruited to helm these profitable pictures, most of the films were written, directed, and produced by whites. In fact, of the 200 blaxploitation films made that starred black actors and an African-American derived story line, fewer than one-fifth were under black control. The white-controlled films, often made with little money and technical expertise, were shot to make an easy profit by exploiting the black audience's need to see black heroes on film. In this regard, the label of "blaxploitation" was fitting.

In response to the deluge of blaxploitation movies being made, black director Michael Schultz created *Cooley High*, released in 1975. Absent of bravado, sexual prowess, prostitution, or pushers, the low-budget film still managed to connect with the blaxploitation era audience. Set in early 1960s Chicago, the black teen comedy-drama focuses on two black high school friends. Cochise, played by Lawrence Hilton-Jacobs, is Cooley High's star basketball player, popular with the girls and a leader of the pack. Preach, played by Glynn Turman, is the exact opposite of Cochise. The bespectacled, skinny teen is shy around the girls, but his intelligence carries him through. The two young men do their share of partying, skipping class, and joking around, until their youthful spirit and carefree existence is shattered by tragedy.

Director Michael Schultz, who would go on to become one of the decade's most productive black filmmakers, successfully mixed humor and frivolities with poignant, tear-jerking drama in *Cooley High*. The film provided the viewer with a glimpse of black teen life in the early 1960s, but more importantly, it offered an alternative to the campy blaxploitation pictures of the era.

The production was not Schultz's first attempt at filmmaking. His 1974 film, *Honeybaby, Honeybaby*, which preceded *Cooley High*, had failed at the box office. But in 1976, he again repeated the commercial success of *Cooley High* with *Car Wash*, which depicts a day in the life of workers at a West Coast car wash and includes comedian Richard Pryor in its cast. Other films starring Pryor quickly followed—in 1976, *The Bingo Long Traveling All-Stars and Motor Kings* and in 1977, *Which Way Is Up?* Schultz's last film of the decade was a poorly received 1978 homage to the Beatles in *Sgt. Pepper's Lonely Hearts Club Band*.

By the mid-1970s, the blaxploitation era had begun to wane. Too few of these films offered either the universal themes white people needed in order to identify with the characters or the ethnicity blacks needed to support these films. *The Wiz*, a lavish black musical variation of *The Wizard of Oz*, which starred Diana Ross and Michael Jackson, was released in 1978 by Motown and is considered by some critics to be the swan song of the black-oriented film movement of the 1970s.

The term "blaxploitation" both helped and killed the genre. While many blaxploitation films were box-office successes, they also fueled the public's perception of blacks as over-sexed gangsters, pushers, and thugs. Black community leaders, critics, and black activist and civil rights groups such as the NAACP, the Student Nonviolent Coordinating Committee, and Southern Christian Leadership Conference often criticized the films for their negative portrayals of blacks, including the common depiction of black women as prostitutes. Activists also took offense at the genre's glorification of drugs, the negative portrayal of the American black man and woman, and the refusal to address black oppression in the United States. But regardless of the criticism, black audiences flocked to the movies and revered these men who countered the prevalent media portrayal of such blacks as revolutionaries and militants.

In this respect, the blaxploitation films of the 1970s represent an important aspect of African-American culture, in spite of the era's legitimate criticisms. Rejecting these films completely is a social disservice. Like Stepin Fetchit before, blaxploitation films like *Superfly*, *Foxy Brown*, and *Blacula*, represent an era of the black experience that was necessary in order to propel black films forward, ensuring their cultural survival and future growth in Hollywood.

Blaxploitation films gave black audiences heroes and sheroes—people who fought and beat a system that had stripped them of their dignity and basic freedoms. The genre also created many instant stars. Plucked from obscurity, ex-football players like Jim Brown and Fred "The Hammer" Williamson, became heroes in the eyes of black moviegoers. The two starred together in films like *Three the Hard Way* (1974), which was directed by Gordon Parks Jr. But ultimately black audiences realized they were being patronized and exploited, and by the late 1970s were avoiding the cinemas. By the start of the 1980s, for all intents and purposes, the blaxploitation boom was over. Taking its place was the phenomenon of so-called crossover films—motion pictures that starred blacks with whites.

6

Film School Filmmakers

THE 1980S WAS the decade of the black superstar. In music, such African-American entertainers as Michael Jackson, Prince, and Whitney Houston dominated the industry. Comedian Bill Cosby reigned supreme on television thanks to his NBC sitcom, *The Cosby Show*. Black actors like Louis Gossett Jr., Eddie Murphy, and Danny Glover appealed to both white and black audiences, and were often featured in black-themed movies and in "buddy pictures." Such pairings of black and white buddies seemed to reflect society's need to downplay the existence of racism in America.

In the 1980s, a flood of films that paired black and white men hit theaters across the country. The 1982 film *An Officer and a Gentleman* featured Louis Gossett Jr. as the tough-talking drill sergeant who shows Richard Gere how to become a man of character. (Gossett won an Oscar for his portrayal.) Eddie Murphy's first film, *48 Hours* (1982), paired him with white actor Nick Nolte. Cast as a convict, Murphy is released from jail for two days to help a white cop catch a killer. A year later, Murphy appeared in *Trading Places*, with white comedian Dan Akroyd. Murphy plays a street hustler who

One of today's most respected filmmakers, Spike Lee (left) performs in his film Do the Right Thing *with veteran actor Ossie Davis.*

61

Sidney Poitier has starred in and directed interracial films that pair blacks with whites, from starring opposite Tony Curtis in The Defiant Ones *to directing Gene Wilder and Richard Pryor in* Stir Crazy.

trades places with a stockbroker at the command of two billionaire brothers who have made a bet about the importance of heredity versus the importance of environment. Another buddy movie was *Lethal Weapon*, released in 1987, in which Mel Gibson and Danny Glover starred as two disparate cops—Gibson suicidal and brash, Glover placating and level-headed—who must balance each other out in order to function.

These interracial films suggested that race was no longer an issue in America, while in fact, racism was still alive and well within society, and certainly in Hollywood. But attempts to address the need for change were imminent as a whole new generation of African-American filmmakers was honing its craft at major film schools across the country.

Jamaa Fanaka was one of the first black members of the film school generation to break through professionally. A summa cum laude graduate of the University of California at Los Angeles (UCLA), Fanaka's first two features, *Welcome Home, Brother Charles* and *Emma Mae*, were film school projects that he parlayed into legitimate feature-film releases in 1975 and 1976, respectively. Fanaka made *Brother Charles* with school grants and released it through Crown International; then he used a $10,000 American Film Institute grant and $4,000 from UCLA's Black Studies Center as seed money to get backing from PRO International on the $250,000 *Emma Mae*.

When Jamaa Fanaka was a child, it was a given that he would direct movies someday, even before his family moved when he was 12 to Compton, California, from his birthplace in Mississippi. As an undergraduate at UCLA, Fanaka's two films paved the way for his masterpiece, *Penitentiary*, a low-budget prison

film that he wrote, produced, and directed using grant money and family savings. Released in 1979, *Penitentiary* was made for a total cost of $600,000 and went on to gross $32 million worldwide. It told the story of convicts at war among themselves and of a young man—falsely imprisoned—who tries to maintain both dignity and sanity in the violently chaotic and almost inhumane environment.

Fanaka hit the European film festival circuit with *Penitentiary* and subsequently signed with MGM/UA to make *Penitentiary II* (1982), and later *Penitentiary III* (1987). Fanaka regretted having made the sequels, he explained in an interview with the *Los Angeles Times* in 1988: "It put me into the category of a prison film maker." His words were prophetic, as the *Penitentiary* films would diminish Hollywood's view of him as a filmmaker in any other genre.

Sidney Poitier's Hollywood ride would be less bumpy. The successful actor continued to direct films in the 1980s, beginning with *Stir Crazy* (1980), a comedy that starred Gene Wilder and Richard Pryor as two out-of-work New Yorkers who are thrown in jail

Gene Wilder (left) looks worried as a police officer frisks Richard Pryor in the film Stir Crazy. *The movie was one of the most successful films directed by Sidney Poitier.*

after being falsely accused of a bank robbery. Comedy ensues as the hapless duo must learn to adapt to their surroundings, including a warden with a short fuse, steely guards, and a multitude of stereotypical inmates. Although the film was dismissed by the critics, it became the number three top grossing film of 1981, and as *Time* magazine reported, "the most successful comedy in industry history." With *Stir Crazy*, Pryor and Wilder introduced the decade's first interracial comedy duo, the first of the buddy picture genre that became popular during the 1980s and 1990s.

Poitier's later directing efforts included guiding Wilder and his wife Gilda Radner in the comedy *Hanky Panky* (1982) and in *Fast Forward* (1985), a story about a group of break-dancing kids. The latter film reflected a new music genre that began to make a tremendous impact in the mid-1980s.

That music was the popular hip-hop—the art of talking to a beat—and its corresponding subculture of break-dancing, graffiti, and slang. Started in the Bronx in the late 70s—hip-hop hit the film industry full force and by the mid-80s had not only inspired Poitier's *Fast Forward* but also other films by white directors—*Beat Street* (1984), *Breakin'* (1984), *Body Rock* (1984), and *Rappin'* (1985). In 1985, African-American director Michael Schultz followed up his comedy hits of the 1970s with *Krush Groove*, featuring the hottest rappers of the genre, including Run-DMC, Kurtis Blow, the Fat Boys, and a skinny, teen-aged LL Cool J. The plot, about the financial troubles of an ambitious young stage manager played by Blair Underwood, often took a backseat to long stretches of concert footage.

Three years before *Krush Groove* was released, New York University film student Spike Lee was basking in the glow of accolades for his student film project, *Joe's Bed-Stuy Barbershop: We Cut Heads* (1982). The student film was screened for the public as part of a New Directors/New Films festival at the Museum of

Modern Art in New York, and eventually was shown at various film festivals around the country.

As a result of the film's popularity, Lee received offers of representation by two talent agencies, William Morris and International Creative Management (ICM). He eventually rebuffed both, finding that they were unable to secure work for him in the film industry. Yet despite the agency hurdle, Lee was well on his way to becoming one of the most acclaimed—and controversial—new filmmakers in Hollywood history.

Born on March 20, 1957, in Atlanta, Georgia, as Shelton Jackson Lee, Spike Lee grew up in the Fort Greene section of Brooklyn, the son of Bill Lee, an accomplished jazz bassist, and Jacquelyn Shelton Lee, an art teacher. When his father could not generate enough income as a bass player to sustain the family, Spike's mother began working as a schoolteacher to make ends meet. She died of cancer in 1976, when Spike was a student at Atlanta's Morehouse College. Following his father and grandfather, Spike was the third generation of Lees to attend Morehouse.

As a mass communications major, Lee took a variety of journalism, radio, and television classes, and he worked at the radio station as well as for the school paper. During his final years at Morehouse, he developed an interest in filmmaking.

In the fall of 1979, Lee enrolled in a three-year graduate film school program at New York University. His first project, a short film entitled *The Answer* (1980), told the story of a black filmmaker given a multimillion-dollar grant to remake D. W. Griffith's *Birth of a Nation*. Lee's film was met with severe criticism by the faculty, whose members accused him of not knowing proper film "grammar" or structure.

Despite the criticism, the school allowed Lee to return for his second year, this time with a teaching

Independent filmmaker Robert Townsend (right) used satire in his film Hollywood Shuffle *to expose the stereotypical roles regularly offered to black actors and actresses.*

assistantship, a job that provided him with access to the film equipment room. During this second year, Lee hooked up with fellow black film student Ernest Dickerson, who served as cameraman for Spike's second-year film, *Sarah*, in 1981. It was followed with his hour-long master's thesis film, *Joe's Bed-Stuy Barbershop: We Cut Heads*. The film, about a small-time betting operation run out of a barbershop, established Lee as a talented director and Dickerson as a skilled cinematographer.

In July 1985, Lee began shooting an independently produced film, *She's Gotta Have It* (1986), with very little money to finance it. In what Lee has described as "guerrilla filmmaking," the shooting was completed in only 12 days. Lee edited the film in his own tiny apartment on a rented editing machine. Released in the spring of 1986, the $175,000 film eventually grossed $8 million at the box office, while generating even more attention for the young filmmaker. Hollywood had no choice but to take Lee seriously: he had made an inexpensive film acclaimed by audiences and critics of all races, and it had created a generous profit.

Lee went on to direct films practically on an annual basis. *School Daze* (1988) reflected his own college experiences at Morehouse. *Do the Right Thing* (1989), which featured a black and white cast dealing with racially explosive situations, earned him an Oscar nomination for Best Original Screenplay. His fifth film, *Jungle Fever* (1991), which starred Wesley Snipes and Samuel L. Jackson, a tale of interracial romance provided social commentary on African-American and white society in terms of class and skin color. The film earned more than twice its $14 million budget.

Lee signed up a star-studded cast for *Malcolm X* (1992), including Denzel Washington and Angela

Financed with credit cards and the help of his friends, Robert Townsend completed Hollywood Shuffle with $100,000. The Samuel Goldwyn Company agreed to distribute the film.

Bassett for the production, which turned out to be, in one reviewer's words, "a surprisingly measured and intelligent portrait of a still controversial figure from his life on the streets to a national leader." Actor/director Ossie Davis, who had appeared in four of Lee's earlier films, played a part in *Malcolm X*, reading the eulogy he'd delivered in real life at the black leader's funeral.

Some of Spike Lee's other films include *Clockers* (1995), *He Got Game* (1998), *Get on the Bus* (1996), and *Summer of Sam* (1999). Lee's journey through Hollywood's rough waters would come to inspire the younger wave of filmmakers who were still cultivating their talent in film school. Like Lee, these filmmakers would use their movies to make social statements.

Keenan Ivory Wayans's film
I'm Gonna Git You Sucka
*poked fun at the blaxploitation
films of the 1970s. Wayans
later became better known as
the creator of the sketch comedy television show* In Living
Color.

As Lee was shooting *School Daze*, another independent black film-maker, Robert Townsend, released a biting satire on the treatment of minorities in Hollywood. Townsend's *Hollywood Shuffle* (1987) was an episodic film lampooning the dilemmas facing black actors and actresses in an industry that offered mainly stereotypical roles, typically gang leaders and thugs. Like Lee's early films, *Hollywood Shuffle* was filmed with the money Townsend raised himself. In fact, he used his credit cards to cover the costs of the filming, which was completed in 14 days for $100,000. He used his credit card again to rent a theater so that the film could be screened before representatives from the major motion picture studios. The Samuel Goldwyn Company agreed not only to distribute the film but also to pay off his huge credit card bills. Townsend followed up Hollywood Shuffle with the 1991 film, *The Five Heartbeats*, in which he documents the rise and fall of an invented singing group.

The early box-office successes of Spike Lee and Robert Townsend made it easier for other black filmmakers to get the major film studios to finance their projects. Townsend's co-screenwriter on *Hollywood Shuffle*, Keenan Ivory Wayans, would eventually emerge as a writer-filmmaker in his own right. After the success of *Hollywood Shuffle*, Wayans was determined to make a name for himself with his 1988 directorial debut, *I'm Gonna Git You Sucka*, a spoof of the black action heroes of the 1970s.

Wayans cast himself in the lead role of Jack Spade, a veteran who returns home when his brother June Bug dies from wearing too many gold chains. The $3 million film went on to gross over $15 million in U.S. theaters, making Wayans Hollywood's next hot black filmmaker. In 1990 Wayans created *In Living Color*, a Fox television comedy show. Employing several of his ten siblings, as well as comedian Jim Carrey, Wayans made the show a Sunday night hit and later an Emmy Award winner.

Other black filmmakers found success portraying black suburban teen life. In 1990 filmmaking brothers Reginald and Warrington Hudlin stomped into the industry with their first feature, *House Party*, a comedy about a teenager's quest to attend the biggest house party of the school year. A crossover film that appealed to black and white youth, the film was made on a $2.5 million budget. *House Party* earned a total of $27 million, quickly solidifying the reputation of the Hudlin brothers as bankable filmmakers.

The filmmaking duo of the Hudlin brothers was another significant film school product. Born in East St. Louis, Missouri, younger brother Reggie attended Harvard University while Warrington went to Yale. During his years at Yale, Warrington developed a desire to make socially conscious films after seeing a screening of Melvin Van Peebles 1971 film, *Sweet Sweetback's Baad Asssss Song*. After graduation, Warrington shot several documentaries, including *Black at Yale* (1974), and *Street Corner Stories* (1977).

Meanwhile, Reggie studied filmmaking at Harvard, showing a talent for fiction and comedy through his early films, *Reggie's World of Soul*, in 1985 and *The Kold Waves* in 1986. His thesis film was called *House Party*, inspired by the Luther Vandross song "Bad Boy/Having a Party." The 20-minute short featured a teenager who wants to join his friends at a party that his father forbids him from attending.

Warrington and Reggie officially became a team in 1986, first directing music videos. The two would take turns directing and writing until Reggie eventually became the primary writer. When *House Party* screened at the Sundance Film Festival in Utah, it

Boyz N the Hood, featuring Ice Cube (right), is a gripping tale of life on the streets of east Los Angeles and was the highest grossing film of 1991.

garnered a positive response from the predominantly white audience. The Hudlin brothers rode this success into other projects such as Eddie Murphy's hit *Boomerang* (1992).

A film school graduate from UCLA who had showed promise as early as 1977 was Charles Burnett. He had grabbed the industry's attention at that time with *Killer of Sheep*, a film about the alienation of a black worker who slowly loses touch with his family and the community. But it wasn't until 1990 that Burnett directed his first feature-length film to be distributed on a nationwide basis. *To Sleep with Anger* starred Danny Glover as a family friend who ultimately disrupts the lives of his hosts. More critical acclaim followed in 1995 with *The Glass Shield*, a gripping police drama about the first black man assigned to a racist and corrupt office of the Los Angeles Police Department.

Charles Burnett's movies, which have spanned three decades, usually center on the everyday lives in black families and communities. A multitalented filmmaker, Burnett has often produced, directed, written, edited, and filmed his own, very distinctive work.

A University of Southern California (USC) film school student who would receive great acclaim was John Daniel Singleton. While at USC, Singleton impressed his professors with his screenplays, and he won several top writing honors, including the Robert Riskin Award and two Jack Nicholson Writing Awards for feature-length screenplays.

Director John Singleton created a name for himself as one of the most prolific young directors in Hollywood. His works have included Boyz N the Hood, Higher Learning, Rosewood, *and his recent remake of* Shaft.

After graduation the aspiring filmmaker took a job as a script reader for Columbia, where his boss agreed to read his screenplay for *Boyz N the Hood*, a story of guns and violence in a black ghetto neighborhood of Los Angeles. She was so impressed that she passed the story along to several talent agencies. The Creative Artists Agency signed him to a contract, and the script eventually made its way across the desk of Stephanie Allain, an African-American vice president at Columbia Pictures. The studio agreed to make the film.

Singleton had to fight against the tradition of studios hiring veteran directors to bring scripts to the screen. The young writer knew that no one could interpret his vision the way he could. Columbia's chairman at the time, Frank Price, took a leap of faith and decided to allow Singleton to become a first-time director. The studio handed Singleton $6 million to shoot the picture, and they also signed him to a lucrative three-year contract that allowed him to make as many films as he wanted during the period.

The Hughes Brothers' Menace II Society *took a tough look at life growing up in the streets. Allen and Albert Hughes began their career filming videos for rappers such as Tupac Shakur before moving on to feature-length films.*

Released in 1991, *Boyz N the Hood* starred Cuba Gooding Jr., Laurence Fishburne, and Angela Bassett. It went on to gross roughly $56 million, making it the highest netting film of the year. The script was nominated for an Academy Award for Best Screenplay, and writer-director John Singleton became the youngest filmmaker and the first African American to be nominated for an Oscar for Best Director.

Singleton's next two films, *Poetic Justice* (1993), with singer Janet Jackson and rapper Tupac Shakur, and *Higher Learning* (1995), which starred Omar Epps and Laurence Fishburne, were unable to generate as much revenue and critical acclaim as *Boyz*. His next film, *Rosewood*, was a fact-based story of a Florida town in the 1920s where racism threatens to destroy an established black community. Released in 1997, the film was met with critical acclaim, but audiences failed to respond at the box office.

Singleton's next feature was a revival of the 1970s blaxploitation staple, *Shaft*. The new film, by the same name, was released in 2000 and starred Samuel L. Jackson in the detective role first made famous by Richard Roundtree.

In addition to his own directorial projects, Singleton has also developed other projects through his production company, New Deal Productions. He served as executive producer on the Daisy V. S. Mayer-directed 1998 comedy *Woo*, which starred Jada Pinkett Smith and Tommy Davidson.

Following in the footsteps of John Singleton were twin brothers who set the industry on its ear with their disturbing directorial debut, *Menace II Society* (1993). Allen and Albert Hughes directed the stark urban tale of what could happen when one falls victim to the violence of the inner city. The main character, Caine, a teenage drug dealer who is tough yet also aware of the bleak future that his Watts, Los Angeles, neighborhood has to offer. Sadly, he is ultimately unable to step back from the drugs, violence, and guns that lure him.

In a review of the film, *Movieline* magazine noted that it "embodied everything that is frightening and out-of-control in our cities." By portraying black teens in an inner-city wasteland, the brothers realistically showed the lifestyle and lack of options available to the inner-city youth.

In real life, Allen and Albert were products of a similar environment yet were able to detach themselves from their gang-influenced southern California home of Pomona. Born in Detroit, the two relocated to Pomona with their Armenian mother when they were nine. Their fascination with violent themes also came from their early years spent in the ghettos of Detroit, and the thoughts of what their lives might have become had they stayed.

One of the few black filmmaking teams not to emerge from film school during the time, the Hughes brothers became interested in making movies when their mother bought them a video camera at age 12. In their early teens, they filmed music videos for such rappers as Tone-Loc and Tupac Shakur. In 1995 Albert and Allen Hughes followed *Menace II Society* with a Vietnam-era heist film called *Dead Presidents*.

7

Youth Music Film

THE YEAR 1991 was a prolific one for black filmmakers. That year Hollywood studios released more than a dozen films created by black directors. Among the new directors was Mario Van Peebles, the son of Melvin Van Peebles and a Columbia University graduate. He had debuted as an actor at the age of 14, when he appeared in the opening scene of his father's 1971 feature *Sweet Sweetback's Baad Asssss Song.* Mario Van Peebles later earned parts in such films as *Rappin'* (1985), *Heartbreak Ridge* (1986), and *Jaws: The Revenge* (1987).

But Mario launched his career behind the camera with the 1991 urban drama *New Jack City.* The antidrug film, which included a score of gangsta rap music, starkly depicted ghetto life and the violence resulting from dealing crack cocaine. Not only did it feature stars like Wesley Snipes and Vanessa Williams, but it also included rappers like Ice-T and Queen Latifah in its cast.

Two films of 1991, John Singleton's *Boyz N the Hood* and Mario Van Peebles's *New Jack City* became two of the top-grossing movies directed by black filmmakers. The films, which each earned more than $50 million, introduced a film genre at the beginning of the 1990s later referred to as "New Jack

One of the top-grossing films by a black filmmaker, New Jack City showcased black performers such as Chris Rock (left) and Ice-T.

Mario Van Peebles followed in the footsteps of his father, Melvin, when he directed the film New Jack City. *The success of the movie opened the door for a wave of black filmmakers.*

Cinema"—films that addressed African-American cultural and social problems in the cities.

The wave of gritty urban dramas, or "hood movies" of the New Jack Cinema of the early 1990s offered an insightful peek into the lives of the disenfranchised in the inner city. An integral part of these urban stories were its characters, often played by controversial rap stars such as Ice-T, Ice Cube, and Tupac Shakur. In film, these artists became the Hollywood equivalent of the subjects they rhymed about on their rap albums. New Jack Cinema films contained powerful images of life in the urban cities: low-income housing, high caliber weapons, and young people with problems.

Still, the New Jack Cinema era coexisted peacefully with the Sidney Poitier of the '90s—Will Smith, who himself had gotten his start as a rap superstar. Smith's success in hip-hop music helped him cross the media boundaries from record albums to film. Later paired with white actors in a series of box-office hits, Smith continued the Hollywood phenomenon known as the buddy picture.

Born and raised in West Philadelphia, Will Smith started rapping when he was 12 and shortly thereafter teamed up with Jeff Townes to become the rap duo Jazzy Jeff and the Fresh Prince. Smith had earned the nickname "Prince" from his elementary school teachers because of his smooth-talking ways. Known for his PG-rated rap lyrics, the Fresh Prince soon became a Grammy-winning musician, as well as the star of the long-running television situation comedy *Fresh Prince of Bel Air*. The show, which began in 1990, ran for six successful years, and in 1993, led to Smith's first starring role in the blockbuster film *Six Degrees of Separation*, in which he offers a subtle performance as a charming con man who convinces a wealthy, gullible New York couple that he is the son of Sidney Poitier.

With critical praise for the role under his belt, Smith next teamed up with Martin Lawrence in the action comedy *Bad Boys* (1995). The film was a box-office hit, boosting Smith's asking price to $5 million per film. He subsequently starred in several 1990s buddy picture megahits—in *Independence Day* (1996) opposite Jeff Goldblum, with Tommy Lee Jones in *Men in Black* (1997), in *Enemy of the State* (1998) opposite Gene Hackman, and with Kevin Kline in *Wild Wild West* (1999).

In the 1980s, foreseeing the success of the rap and hip-hop music genre in film, black producer Doug McHenry had joined forces with George Jackson to form Jackson-McHenry Entertainment. After producing the groundbreaking youth music-oriented *Krush Groove*, the company went on to produce the impressive gangster epic *New Jack City* and the hip-hop hits *House Party 2* and *House Party 3*. All three of these films reflected the era's new fascination with hip-hop music, featuring rappers in leading roles and star-studded rap soundtracks.

Having made his directorial debut with *House Party 2*, Doug McHenry next directed the critically acclaimed *Jason's Lyric* in 1994. The drama starred

In Carwash Mr. B (Sully Boyar, left) fires Duane (Bill Duke, right) for being late for work. Duke's experience in front of the camera would lead to a career behind the camera in both film and TV work.

Allen Payne as Jason—a dependable workingman in love with a waitress named Lyric, but struggling with how to handle his drug-addicted brother.

Raised in Oakland and Danville, California, McHenry earned a bachelor of arts in economics and political science from Stanford University and graduate degrees in both law and business administration from Harvard. While studying for the California bar exam, Doug took a position as executive assistant to Peter Guber, then head of Casablanca Records/Filmworks, where he assumed responsibility for both production and business affairs. After moving on to AVCO/Embassy Pictures, McHenry worked as an executive on films such as *Midnight Express*, *Foxes*, *Escape from New York*, and *Time Bandits*.

McHenry's business partner, Harvard-educated George Jackson, grew up in Harlem and began his career as a producer trainee at Paramount Studios. He gained hands-on experience working on television shows like *Laverne and Shirley* and *The New Odd*

Danny Glover wields a handgun in a scene from Bill Duke's A Rage in Harlem. *Duke began his career as an actor, appearing in a number of successful films such as* Predator *and* Commando.

Couple, which featured black leading men in the original *Odd Couple* roles of Felix and Oscar. Jackson later became president of production at Richard Pryor's production company, Indigo. While at Indigo, Jackson worked with such up-and-coming filmmakers as Reginald Hudlin, Spike Lee, and Robert Townsend.

In 1997 Jackson was named president and chief executive of Motown Records, where he oversaw such acts as the Temptations and the boy band 98°. After leaving Motown, Jackson established the Urban Box Office (UBO) network, described as a "next generation" media company providing an interactive platform for the "urban mindset."

Another African-American director of major significance in the early 1990s was Bill Duke, a respected actor who had starred in such films as *Car Wash* (1976) opposite Sully Boyar, *Commando* (1985) and *Predator* (1987) opposite Arnold Schwarzenegger, and *Bird on a Wire* (1990) opposite Mel Gibson and Goldie Hawn. When he wasn't acting, Duke was

From left to right: Loretta Devine, Lela Rochon, Angela Bassett, and Whitney Houston in a scene from Waiting to Exhale, *directed by Forest Whitaker.*

usually tinkering behind the scenes, and eventually directed episodes for television programs like *Hill Street Blues, Miami Vice, Cagney and Lacey,* and *Dallas.* In 1984, Duke directed a feature-length film for public television called *The Killing Floor,* which told the story of black slaughterhouse workers in Chicago and their efforts to form a union after World War I.

In 1991, Duke made his feature film directorial debut with *A Rage in Harlem,* adapted from the novel by Chester Himes. Bill Duke was selected for this position because the producers specifically wanted a black director with both the cultural background and filmmaking experience needed to bring Himes's Harlem setting to life. Although the film failed financially, it earned critical acclaim as Duke's directorial debut. New Line Cinema subsequently signed him to direct the police thriller *Deep Cover* (1992), which starred Laurence Fishburne as an undercover narcotics agent. Duke then went on to direct such films as *The Cemetery Club* (1993), a film about three widowed Jewish women, and *Sister Act 2: Back in the Habit* (1993), which starred Whoopi Goldberg.

Forest Whitaker had been one of the coproducers of *A Rage in Harlem*, and had helped ensure that Bill Duke had been at the helm of that project. Whitaker later made his own directorial debut with the cable network HBO in the urban drama *Strapped* (1993), a story of a teenager growing up in Brooklyn housing projects. The film earned Whitaker the award of Best New Director at the Toronto Film Festival.

Whitaker went on to direct the film adaptation of Terry McMillan's best-selling novel *Waiting to Exhale*, a tale of black women and their relationships with men. Released in 1995, the black-themed film included Whitney Houston and Angela Bassett in its cast.

Forest Whitaker made a name for himself as both an actor and director. His 1995 film Waiting to Exhale *immediately made him one of the most sought after talents in directing.*

Three years later Whitaker worked with actress Sandra Bullock directing the film *Hope Floats*, which featured an all-white cast.

Bullock's collaboration with Whitaker proved to be as much of an opportunity for her to earn acceptance as a major Hollywood player crossing gender lines as it was for him crossing racial lines. Bullock served as a first-time executive-producer of the film, and for Whitaker, flush with the success of *Waiting to Exhale*, it was a chance to refine his hand at tragedy. In *Hope Floats*, the story of a woman learning to cope after discovering her husband's adultery, Whitaker subtly conveys the woman's slow emotional unraveling, as she tries to learn how to come to terms with herself.

Meanwhile New Jack Cinema directors found success by capitalizing on hip-hop culture, making films that feature eclectic casts of cultural icons, hip-hop stars, and athletes, accompanied by a pounding hip-hop soundtrack in the tradition of *New Jack City*. From the beginning of this hip-hop genre, white kids have been at least as devoted to rap as black kids, and the films have helped fuel the white, suburban obsession with rap and its corresponding culture. From the Jackson/McHenry era of *New Jack City* and the *House Party* films through the brutal honesty of the hip-hop-influenced *Boyz N the Hood* and *Menace II Society* in the 1990s, the genre has proven to be a powerful one.

Even with the ability of Bill Duke, Forest Whitaker, and the host of New Jack directors to bring their vision to the big screen, there was still one voice unable to break through. Jamaa Fanaka, the director of all three *Penitentiary* movies, had been trying for years to leave the jailhouse movies behind, only to be stopped cold by the indifference of Hollywood. During the 1980s and 1990s, he saw the success of university-trained filmmakers such as Spike Lee and John Singleton, and like them wanted to direct films in other subject matter as well, but no major distributors would back him.

Fanaka couldn't understand why his summa cum laude UCLA background, coupled with the successes of his three *Penitentiary* films would not open doors for him. "With the good reviews I got on 'Penitentiary III' . . . the average white [filmmaker] could take those reviews and get the best agent and go on to their next film," Fanaka noted in a 1988 *Los Angeles Times* interview. "With me, it's not so easy. I think ultimately I'm going to succeed. I refuse to fail."

In 1997, Fanaka took more than 20 major motion picture and television companies to task in a $1.5 billion class action lawsuit over alleged discriminatory hiring practices. Fanaka claimed he had applied for 2,820 writing, directing, and production jobs in the last two years and had yet to receive one job offer. "The system is set up to keep out not only blacks, but everyone without connections," Fanaka told the Los Angeles Times in 1997. "When the system changes and really opens up, it will not only benefit the minorities—it will open it up to a genuine democratic situation where everybody has a chance."

8

Beyond Urban Cinema

On many critics' lists of the
best pictures of 1997, Eve's
Bayou tells the story of a
dysfunctional family and their
struggles in the Creole-flavored
countryside of Louisiana.
Here, Roz Batiste, played by
Lynne Whitfield, consoles her
daughter Eve, played by Jurnee
Smollett.

TECHNOLOGY IS THE force that gave birth to
the film industry, and it has been the newest
technologies that have continued to usher in each
new crop of filmmakers. "Technology is really
developing in a way that supports diversity," says
independent film producer/director Doug McHenry. "As the quality of video, digital cameras, etc.
continues to go up, the cost of making a film will
come down. It will give more people the ability to
make films, and hopefully we will have greater
diversity. That's why new technology supports our
independence."

Now at the beginning of the 21st century, the
film industry finds itself being bombarded with black
actors, athletes, and rappers—all creating films
under the auspices of their own production companies, and all eager to tell their own stories. A change
in the role of black filmmakers is also taking place,
as they begin to tell stories outside of their own culture. Through special programs film companies are
also starting to provide more opportunities to
minorities. Yet with all of these important advances,
the racism woven into the historical fabric of the
American film industry remains.

The success of two independently made films, Spike Lee's *She's Gotta Have It*, released in 1986, and Robert Townsend's *Hollywood Shuffle*, released a year later, was a catalyst in cracking open the Hollywood door for other independent black filmmakers to get their films to the big screen. Soon, inner-city youths who had found success in the rap game began to dominate the big screen in New Jack Cinema. Following in the footsteps of Will Smith, rap stars LL Cool J, Queen Latifah, and Heavy D easily made the leap from rapping to acting.

One of the most prolific and respected lyricists in hip-hop, Ice Cube also brought the intensity of his gangsta-rhymes to the field of acting. Cube took the leap one step further—to call his own shots behind the camera as well. His journey is a classic example of how rappers are able to successfully maneuver their entrepreneurial spirit from recording to celluloid.

Ice Cube, also known as O'Shea Jackson, was born in South Central Los Angeles. Despite having parents who were both professors at UCLA, Ice Cube spent his teen years surrounded by the pervasive gang subculture that permeated the entire inner city. After finding success as part of the groundbreaking gangsta rap group NWA, he pursued an even more successful solo career, eventually starting his own record company, Street Knowledge, and becoming one of the major players in hip-hop. During this period, first-time director John Singleton tapped him in 1991 to play a role in *Boyz N the Hood*. While the film earned Singleton both screenwriting and directing Oscar nominations, Cube also received praise for his stark portrayal of Dough Boy, the neighborhood boy who can't escape the gang lifestyle that surrounds him.

Ice Cube's Hollywood appeal landed him roles in several more films, including Singleton's *Higher Learning* and the killer-snake horror flick *Anaconda*. He went on to cowrite the box-office hit *Friday*, and in 1998 made his directorial debut with *The Player's Club*, which he also wrote. Although both films were

dismissed by the critics, each generated major revenue, which solidified Ice Cube's reputation for being able to attract theater audiences.

In a March 2000 cover story for the *Los Angeles Times* magazine entitled, "Empire Builders: New Rules, New Players in 21st Century Hollywood," Ice Cube expressed a desire that his new production company, Cubevision, would help create even more opportunities for younger black filmmakers: "I hope that happens so that someday they can make movies. And then," he added, "they can give me a role in them."

Master P is another rapper who has been able to parlay his successful record label into an empire that includes ventures not only in film but also in television, new media, toys, clothing, and sports management. In December 1999, the rapper's film production company, No Limit Films inked a multipicture deal with Trimark Pictures that will finance several projects. Trimark will fund a minimum of five No Limit

Another rapper who turned his attention to films is Ice Cube (right), who wrote and starred in the highly successful Friday. *Like many other black filmmakers, Ice Cube also created his own production studio.*

Director Julie Dash, with four films to her credit, has done much to advance the position of female minority directors in Hollywood.

films and will then help to market and distribute them. Master P and No Limit Films have already been able to build a loyal audience through the release of straight-to-video films such as *I'm Bout It* and *Lock Down*. The success of *I'm Bout It* led to the theatrical release for *No Tomorrow* (1998) and *Hot Boyz* (1999).

Rappers are not the only entrepreneurs who have taken advantage of Hollywood's slowly opening door. Comedian Martin Lawrence was able to parlay his successful stand-up comedy and television career into film, landing in the director's chair for the comedy-thriller *A Thin Line Between Love and Hate* (1996), also written by and starring Lawrence. The film, backed by Jackson-McHenry at a cost of less than $10 million, grossed more than $36 million within six weeks of its release. *Thin Line* was an important film in that it bucked the trend of hood movies that had begun to inundate screens across America in the wake of Singleton's and the Hughes brothers' successes.

In *A Thin Line Between Love and Hate*, Lawrence plays Darnell Wright, a playboy who is always on the prowl. After he sets his sights on the sophisticated Brandi Web, played by Lynn Whitfield, he goes all out to win her over. When he finally does, Brandi proves much harder to shake than she was to get, especially when she realizes she has a rival in Mia, played by Regina King, a childhood friend who has a

thing for Darnell as well. When Darnell puts his foot down with Brandi and chooses Mia, an obsessed Brandi begins stalking the new love of her life.

By 1996, films backed by Jackson-McHenry were consistently grossing nearly twice the industry average for similarly budgeted films. Doug McHenry took advantage of this success to cofound and become chairman of Elephant Walk Entertainment, and he created several entities under the company umbrella. The new firms included Elephant Walk Television, Elephant Walk Management, and Elephant Walk Records, as well as the music publishing companies Harlem Boys Music and Oaktown Boys Music. When George Jackson left to become the president of Motown Records, McHenry ran the Elephant Walk Entertainment companies with partner Rob Lee.

A shortage of trained female directors remains a problem in the filmmaking industry, as black women still have a difficult time trying to combat sexist attitudes within a male-dominated industry. One woman

Gina Prince-Bythewood (left) with Sanaa Lathan on the set of Love and Basketball. *This was Bythewood's third film and it won critical acclaim at the prestigious Sundance Film Festival in 2000.*

who has helped immensely to soften up Hollywood's acceptance of the female minority is Julie Dash. The powerful film *Daughters of the Dust* (1991), coproduced, written, and directed by Dash, tells the story of the Peazant family, descendants of slaves living on islands near South Carolina who have maintained their African traditions. As the Peazant family prepares to move north, its members are at odds about how important their traditions and customs will be to their new lifestyle. Nana Peazant, the 88-year-old matriarch of the family, believes that the old rituals, ceremonies, and religious beliefs are the base of the family's stability, and she fights to maintain the family's culture.

Daughters of the Dust earned the UCLA film school graduate critical praise for a film that crossed over to the general public without much promotion. Dash has also been instrumental in bringing the work of other black filmmakers to the attention of the public. At the 1980 Cannes Film Festival, she cosponsored a screening of several short films by black Americans, which led to the historic retrospective of African-American cinema later held at The Forum Les Halles in Paris.

Like Bill Duke and Forest Whitaker, Kasi Lemmons rose to her position as a director after years of proving her mettle first as an actress in television and film. In 1997 she wrote and directed *Eve's Bayou*, set in Louisiana's backwater Creole community during the late 1950s. The story is a coming-of-age tale about two adolescent sisters, the 10-year-old narrator Eve, played by Jurnee Smollett, and her older sister Cisely, played by Meagan Good. When Eve catches her father, Louis,

Talented director Gina Prince-Bythewood received critical acclaim for her film Love and Basketball, *which starred Sanaa Lathan and Omar Epps and was co-produced by Spike Lee.*

played by Samuel L. Jackson, with a neighbor's wife in the wine cellar, the young girl worries that her already dysfunctional family will become unglued because of the affair. Therefore, she decides that some voodoo rituals are in order to save the family. The cast of characters includes Lynn Whitfield as Louis's controlling wife, soap opera star Debbi Morgan as Louis's psychic sister, and Diahann Carroll as a foul fortuneteller. More than anything, Lemmons's film presented a slice of African-American life rarely seen on film.

Film critic Roger Ebert called *Eve's Bayou* one of the best films of 1997. He wrote in the *Chicago Sun Times,* "*Eve's Bayou* will represent a marketing challenge because the Creole and voodoo material will suggest it's a genre picture when in fact it's a legitimate contender for an Oscar nomination for Best Picture."

Lemmons followed up in 2001 with *The Caveman's Valentine,* a well-received murder mystery starring Samuel L. Jackson as Romulus Ledbetter, a recluse who emerges from his cave in Central Park, New York City, to help solve the murder of a homeless youth.

First-time feature filmmaker Gina Prince-Bythewood received critical praise for her film *Love and Basketball* when it was screened at the 2000 Sundance Film Festival. Executives from New Line Cinema who saw the film jumped at the chance to distribute the work of the UCLA film student to a nationwide audience. Produced by Spike Lee and Sam Kitt, the story follows Monica Wright, played by Sanaa Lathan, and Quincy McCall, played by Omar Epps—childhood adversaries and talented athletes who have a love for the game of basketball and each other. Each pursues the dream of basketball success through high school, college, and the pros, but along the way they must face their own personal obstacles.

The success of Prince-Bythewood comes in the wake of other black women in the struggle to be heard in Hollywood. Charlie Jordan, the female director of the short film *One Red Rose*, worked for years for major studios, but believed the only way to bring her voice to the screen was by forming her own independent film company. She had grown frustrated by Hollywood studios, which seemed to view African-American male and female directors as one entity and usually handed off "minority" films to male, rather than female directors.

Hollywood has only recently started to appreciate the wonderful diversity and profitable nature of black filmmakers. Forest Whitaker's 1995 *Waiting to Exhale* was the first to usher in a genre featuring middle-class African-American stories. The film crossed over to white audiences and grossed $72.4 million. After 20th Century Fox saw the success of this new genre, the distributor quickly financed a similar film, directed by George Tillman. Released in 1997, *Soul Food* tells the story of three sisters who are struggling to keep the family together after their mother falls ill. Produced by Tracey Edmonds, wife of producer Babyface Edmonds, the film was a surprise success, generating $43 million in ticket sales.

Hollywood looked to capitalize on films featuring middle-class African Americans, and soon the industry began reaping the benefits with such box-office hits as Theodore Wicher's *Love Jones* (1997) and Rick Famuyi-wa's *The Wood* (1999), as well as Julie Dash's *Daughters of the Dust* and Kasi Lemmons's *Eve's Bayou*, the highest-grossing independent film of 1997. These movies ushered in a new wave of filmmaking that reflected many different facets of the African-American experience, not just the urban inner-city life of New Jack Cinema.

One company at the forefront of cultivating future black filmmaking talent is the cable network Showtime, which strongly supports and showcases the innovative work of aspiring black filmmakers. During the 1990s, Showtime aired the short works of a select group of emerging African-American writers/directors in its *Showtime Black Filmmaker Showcase*. Established to support up-and-coming African-American filmmakers, the showcase included a $30,000 grant to help the selected film-maker produce an original short film, which would premiere exclusively on the network. The grant recipient is also introduced to Showtime's development process and works closely with the network's development executives. Past honorees in the *Showtime Black Filmmaker Showcase* have included Rick Wilkinson, Matty Rich, Leslie Harris, Garrett Williams, Malcolm Lee, Debbi Reynolds, Deborah Pratt, Monice Mitchell, Bobby Mardis, and Nandi Bowe.

As up-and-coming black filmmakers obtain more work in the entertainment industry, writer-producer-director Jamaa Fanaka is still struggling to right the wrongs of a Hollywood he views as severely discriminatory. In December of 1999, an appellate court reversed a district court's decision to dismiss his case, allowing Fanaka to continue his suits against the film companies Time Warner, Walt Disney, Metro-Goldwyn-Mayer, 20th Century Fox, Paramount, Universal Studios, and Dreamworks

THE POWER OF FILM

"When you walk through the doors of a theater . . . you give permission to a total stranger, that filmmaker, those actors, whatever, to *reach* you; there, your defenses are down. You say, make me cry, make me laugh, make me feel something," says filmmaker/producer Doug McHenry. According to him, this is the power of movies. He observes that we don't allow that privilege to many others, certainly not strangers in the street, nor politicians, nor most of the people we meet in our daily activities.

Because the filmmaker has the ability to create a believable world, to shape ideas and attitudes, to make people believe in his or her reality, the power of being a filmmaker carries with it an awesome responsibility. Whatever the filmmaker chooses to depict on the screen holds the ability to penetrate the emotions of human beings.

When someone sits down to watch a movie in a theater, he or she is giving the person who created the film complete trust, an intimacy usually shared only with family and friends. As McHenry notes, "What we reserve for ourselves is the ability to feel with those that we really trust, like with our mothers, our fathers, our kids; the other space that we reserve to feel is in the movie theater, so I think there is a great responsibility."

Doug McHenry advises anyone considering entering the field of filmmaking to understand the potential within his or her hands: "What I would say to a young person—it's not *just* being a filmmaker, it's a great responsibility, because in very few other spaces in our lives do we allow ourselves to be vulnerable like [we are when watching a good film]. So you have to have a mission, and your number one mission is to tell the story, and do as good a job as you can, and above all don't be boring—make people feel something at the end of the experience."

SKG, and against the television networks CBS, NBC, ABC, and Fox.

Even at the end of the 20th century, many African Americans remained discouraged about the lack of the opportunities available to blacks in the entertainment industry, particularly in television. In 1999 the NAACP launched a nationwide campaign to encourage the entertainment industry to include more blacks behind the scenes as writers, producers, and directors in television. The NAACP Television and Film Industry Diversity Initiative has found some success in monitoring and addressing the dearth of black characters on and behind the cameras of prime-time TV.

Meanwhile, a new trend has been developing in the film industry in which black directors have been chosen to steer all-white casts. Bill Duke was perhaps the first to start the trend when he directed the 1993 film *Cemetery Club*, a story about three older Jewish widows. A year later, Thomas Carter helmed *Swing Kids*, which is about German youths obsessed with American swing music.

Forest Whitaker had shocked the producers of the Sandra Bullock film *Hope Floats* when he told them of his interest in directing its all-white cast. Producer Lynda Obst had considered Whitaker an "urban director," citing his work

Don Cheadle points a pistol at Denzel Washington in an intense scene from Devil in a Blue Dress, *directed by Carl Franklin.*

on the HBO film *Strapped* and *Waiting to Exhale*. But when Bullock, Obst, and Whitaker met for the first time, Obst knew she had found the right director to bring the *Hope Floats* story to life. She told the *St. Louis Post-Dispatch*, "He's from Long-view, Texas, a small town; he loved the same scenes that we did; he knew these women and family issues and rhythms. I realized then that it was a non-gender, non-race issue for Forest to direct this movie."

Kevin Hooks first gained recognition for directing *Passenger 57* (1992), with Wesley Snipes, and *Fled* (1996), with Lawrence Fishburne. He was subsequently tapped to direct Universal Studios *Black Dog* (1998), a trucker action drama with a white cast that included Patrick Swayze, Randy Travis, and Meat Loaf.

Carl Franklin has also had success directing all-white casts. Franklin came to film after graduating from the American Film Institute's masters program in 1986. Critics first noted his directing skill in the 1992 film

One False Move, with Bill Paxton, Cynda Williams, and Billy Bob Thornton, made for only $2.2 million. Because the cops and killers in the film featured both black and white actors, many people wrongly assumed Franklin was a white director. With the film's success, Franklin received a wide range a material to direct, thus avoiding being pigeonholed into one genre as often happens to black directors. He followed *One False Move* with a well-received 1940s detective story, *Devil in a Blue Dress* (1995), which starred Denzel Washington.

By the mid-1990s, Franklin was best known for directing the HBO black family miniseries *Laurel Avenue* and for *Devil in a Blue Dress*, but soon afterward followed these efforts with *One True Thing*, a film with an all-white cast. Franklin received critical acclaim for directing Meryl Streep and Renee Zellweger in the 1998 mother-daughter film about a white woman who relinquishes her job as a magazine writer in New York to move home and care for her terminally ill mother. The director said he personally identified with the story because he was like the daughter who underestimated her mother because she was a housewife—he had felt the same way toward his mother. That was before she developed cancer in 1986 and waged an eight-month battle for survival. Franklin recognized that what mattered in telling this story was the human level of its characters, not the color of its family members.

Antoine Fuqua (*The Replacement Killers*, 1998) and F. Gary Gray (*The Negotiator*, 1998) are also black directors who have directed predominantly white casts. Their work symbolizes a further chipping away of the old attitudes of race in the film industry. Perhaps Doug McHenry summed up the trend best: "In the year 2000, we would hope that African-Americans will have more control and freedom to tell the stories we want to tell, be they African American or not."

In December of 1999, the Directors Guild of America decided to retire the name of one of its awards—the prestigious D. W. Griffith Award, which honored outstanding achievements of film directors. D. W. Griffith is probably best remembered for his 1915 epic *Birth of a Nation*—a film with racist themes and negative portrayals of blacks. DGA president Jack Shea noted that the name was retired in order to reflect a sensitivity to race relations and society's changing awareness.

The future for black filmmakers holds many possibilities. Yet the success of today's film directors has resulted from the struggle of past black filmmakers to tell their stories and demonstrate their talents. Whether black directors exercise their dreams within the Hollywood system or independently, they will continue to soar into the future on the wings of those who came before them.

CHRONOLOGY

1888   Thomas Edison patents a motion picture camera, although its film cannot be projected for an audience; through the following years, inventors contribute to the development of motion picture technology

1910   William Foster establishes the first black film company, Foster Photoplay

1915   D. W. Griffith releases the controversial film *The Birth of a Nation*

1916   Actor Noble Johnson and his brother George form the Lincoln Motion Picture Company

1918   Oscar Micheaux forms the Micheaux Film and Book Company; produces and directs his first feature film, *The Homesteader*, based on his book

1920s–30s   In the height of race movies production executives of film companies create hundreds of films targeted to black audiences; Oscar Micheaux is the leading black director

1929   A study reveals that 461 movie theaters across America cater exclusively to black audiences

1938   Hattie McDaniel becomes first African American to win an Oscar in the category of Best Supporting Actress for her role in *Gone with the Wind*

1940s   Production of race movies wanes as filmmaking costs increase; from 1941 to 1947 black actor/director Spencer Williams writes, produces, and directs films especially for black audiences

1963   Sidney Poitier is the first African American to win the Oscar for Best Actor for his role in *Lilies of the Field*

1969   Gordon Parks is the first African American to produce, direct, and score a film for a major Hollywood studio, Warner Brothers; the film *The Learning Tree* is based on Parks's original book by the same name

1971   Melvin Van Peebles makes his directorial debut with *Sweet Sweetback's Baad Asssss Song*, a film that introduces a new, defiant black hero

1979   UCLA film school graduate Jamaa Fanaka directs the critically acclaimed and commercially successful film *Penitentiary*, becoming one of the first

African-American filmmakers of the film school generation to make a professional breakthrough

1980   Sidney Poitier directs *Stir Crazy*, which stars Richard Pryor and Gene Wilder. It sells more than 37 million tickets, becoming the biggest hit film by an African-American director.

1985   Partners George Jackson and Doug McHenry establish Jackson/McHenry Productions, which pioneers the urban music theme in films; produce Michael Schultz–directed *Krush Groove*, the first of the youth-music film genre

1986   Spike Lee releases his film *She's Gotta Have It* and becomes a major inspiration for other African-American directors; black film pioneer Oscar Micheaux is posthumously inducted into the Directors Guild of America

1987   Robert Townsend launches his career as a director with *Hollywood Shuffle*

1990   Reginald Hudlin directs *House Party*, which initiates a series of "party" movies

1991   Director Mario Van Peebles releases *New Jack City*, which ignites a movement referred to as New Jack Cinema; John Singleton is nominated for an Oscar in the Best Director category for *Boyz N the Hood*.

1997   Actress Kasi Lemmons makes directorial debut with critically acclaimed *Eve's Bayou*

1998   Actor and rap superstar Ice Cube adds the craft of filmmaking to his repertoire with his film *The Players Club*

1999   Rap star Master P and his No Limit Films signs a deal with Trimark Pictures

2000   Gina Prince-Bythewood directs film *Love and Basketball*, co-produced by Spike Lee and distributed by New Line Cinema

SELECTED FILMOGRAPHY OF BLACK DIRECTORS

Silent Films

William Foster (1884–1940)
    (Foster Photoplay Company)
    The Pullman Porter (1910)
    The Railroad Porter (1912)
    The Fall Guy (1913)

Independent African-American Filmmakers
    The Birth of a Race (1918)

Noble Johnson (1881–1978)
    (Lincoln Motion Picture Company)
    The Realization of a Negro's Ambition (1916)
    A Trooper of Troop K (1916)
    By Right of Birth (1921)

Oscar Micheaux (1884–1951)
    (Micheaux Film and Book Company, later Micheaux Film Company)
    The Homesteader (1919)
    Within Our Gates (1920)
    Birthright (1924)
    Body and Soul (1925)
    The Spider's Web (1927)
    The Millionaire (1927)
    A Daughter of the Congo (1930)

Sound Films

Oscar Micheaux
    The Exile (1931)
    Murder in Harlem (1935)
    God's Step Children (1938)
    Birthright (1939)
    The Notorious Elinor Lee (1940)
    The Betrayal (1948)

Spencer Williams (1893–1969)
   Blood of Jesus (1941)
   Of One Blood (1944)
   The Girl in Room 20 (1946)
   Beale Street Mama (1947)

Gordon Parks Sr. (1912–   )
   The Learning Tree (1969)
   Shaft (1971)
   Shaft's Big Score! (1972)
   The Super Cops (1974)
   Leadbelly (1976)

Ossie Davis (1917–   )
   Cotton Comes to Harlem (1970)
   Kongi's Harvest (1970)
   Black Girl (1972)
   Gordon's War (1973)
   Countdown at Kusini (1976)

Sidney Poitier (1927–   )
   Buck and the Preacher (1972)
   A Warm December (1973)
   Uptown Saturday Night (1974)
   Let's Do It Again (1975)
   A Piece of the Action (1977)
   Stir Crazy (1980)
   Hanky Panky (1982)
   Fast Forward (1985)
   Ghost Dad (1990)

Melvin Van Peebles (1932–   )
   Watermelon Man (1970)
   Sweet Sweetback's Baad Asssss Song (1971)
   Identity Crisis (1989)
   Bellyful (2000)

SELECTED FILMOGRAPHY OF BLACK DIRECTORS

Gordon Parks Jr. (1934–1979)
Superfly (1972)
Thomasine & Bushrod (1974)
Three the Hard Way (1974)
Aaron Loves Angela (1975)

Michael Schultz (1938–   )
Honeybaby, Honeybaby (1974)
Cooley High (1975)
Car Wash (1976)
Which Way Is Up? (1977)
Sgt. Pepper's Lonely Hearts Club Band (1978)
Krush Groove (1985)

Jamaa Fanaka (1942–   )
Welcome Home, Brother Charles (1975)
Emma Mae (1976)
Penitentiary (1979)
Penitentiary II (1982)
Penitentiary III (1987)
Street Wars (1992)

Mario Van Peebles (1957–   )
New Jack City (1991)
Posse (1993)
Panther (1995)
Love Kills (1998)
Standing Knockdown (1999)

Spike Lee (1957–)
She's Gotta Have It (1986)
School Daze (1988)
Do the Right Thing (1989)
Mo' Better Blues (1990)
Jungle Fever (1991)
Malcolm X (1992)
Crooklyn (1994)
Clockers (1995)
He Got Game (1998)

Get on the Bus (1996)
Summer of Sam (1999)
The Original Kings of Comedy (2000)
Bamboozled (2000)

Robert Townsend (1957–)
Hollywood Shuffle (1987)
The Five Heartbeats (1991)
The Meteor Man (1993)
B*A*P*S (1997)
Fraternity Boys (1999)

Keenan Ivory Wayans (1958–)
I'm Gonna Get You Sucka (1988)
A Low Down Dirty Shame (1994)
Scary Movie (2000)
Scary Movie II (2001)

Reginald Hudlin (1961–)
House Party (1990)
The Great White Hype (1996)
The Ladies Man (2000)

Reginald and Warrington Hudlin
Boomerang (1992)

Charles Burnett (1944–)
Killer of Sheep (1977)
My Brother's Wedding (1984)
To Sleep with Anger (1990)
The Glass Shield (1995)
Finding Buck McHenry (2000)

John Singleton (1968–)
Boys N the Hood (1991)
Poetic Justice (1993)
Higher Learning (1995)
Rosewood (1997)
Shaft (2000)
Baby Boy (2001)

SELECTED FILMOGRAPHY OF BLACK DIRECTORS

The Hughes Brothers: Abert Hughes (1972–   ) and Allen Hughes (1972–   )
Menace II Society (1993)
Dead Presidents (1995)

Doug McHenry (1950–   )
House Party 2 (1991)
Jason's Lyric (1994)
Kingdom Come (2001)

Bill Duke (1943–   )
The Killing Floor (1984)
A Rage in Harlem (1991)
Deep Cover (1992)
The Cemetery Club (1993)
Sister Act 2: Back in the Habit (1993)

Forest Whitaker (1961–   )
Waiting to Exhale (1995)
Hope Floats (1998)

Ice Cube (O'Shea Jackson) (1969–   )
The Players Club (1998)

Master P (Percy Miller) (1969–   )
No Limit Films
I'm Bout It (1997) (Video)
Lock Down (1998) (Video)
No Tomorrow (1998)
Hot Boyz (1999)

Martin Lawrence (1965–   )
A Thin Line Between Love and Hate (1996)

Julie Dash (1952–   )
Praise House (1991)
Daughters of the Dust (1991)
Illusions (1982)
Diary of an African Nun (1977)

SELECTED FILMOGRAPHY OF BLACK DIRECTORS

Kasi Lemmons (1961–   )
   Eve's Bayou (1997)
   The Caveman's Valentine (2001)

Gina Prince-Bythewood (1968–   )
   Stitches (1991)
   Bowl of Pork (1997)
   Love and Basketball (2000)

Kevin Hooks (1958–   )
   Strictly Business (1991)
   Passenger 57 (1992)
   Fled (1996)
   Black Dog (1998)
   Lie Detector (1999)

Carl Franklin (1949–   )
   One False Move (1991)
   Devil in a Blue Dress (1995)
   One True Thing (1998)
   High Crimes (2001)

Antione Fuqua (1966–   )
   The Replacement Killers (1998)
   Bait (2000)

F. Gary Gray (1970–   )
   Friday (1995)
   Set It Off (1996)
   The Negotiator (1998)
   Diablo (2001)

FURTHER READING

Books

Berry, Skip. *Gordon Parks*. New York and Philadelphia: Chelsea House Publishers, 1991.

Ehrlick, Scott. *Paul Robeson*. New York and Philadelphia: Chelsea House Publishers, 1988.

Green, J. Ronald. *Straight Lick: The Cinema of Oscar Micheaux*. Bloomington, Ill.: Indiana University Press, 2000.

Hardy, James Earl. *Spike Lee*. Philadelphia: Chelsea House Publishers, 1996.

Jackson, Carlton. *Hattie: The Life of Hattie McDaniel*. New York: Madison Books, 1990.

Kendall, Steven D. *New Jack Cinema: Hollywood's African-American Filmmakers*. New York: J.L. Denser Publishing, 1996.

Parker, Janice. *Great African-Americans in Film*. New York: Crabtree Publishing, 1997.

Rediger, Pat. *Great African-Americans in Entertainment*. New York: Crabtree Publishing, 1996.

Singleton, John, and Veronica Chambers. *Poetic Justice: Filmmaking South Central Style*. New York: Dell Publishing, 1993.

Websites

Black Film Center: Department of Afro-American Studies at Indiana University
http://www.indiana.edu/~bfca

Black Filmmakers Hall of Fame
http://www.blackfilmmakershall.org

Blaxploitation
http://blaxploitation.com

The Internet Movie Database
http://www.imdb.com

Midnight Ramble/Modern Times (early black cinema classics)
http://www.moderntimes.com/palace/black/index.html

Oscar Micheaux Society
http://www.duke.edu/web/film/Micheaux

The Silents Majority (Black Americans and Silent Film)
http://www.mdle.com/ClassicFilms/SpecialFeature/feb97.htm

INDEX

INDEX

PICTURE CREDITS

COOKIE LOMMEL started her career as a journalist in the entertainment industry. She has interviewed hundreds of film, television,
and music personalities as an on-camera reporter for CNN. Ms. Lommel has written several books for young adults, including biographies
of Madame C. J. Walker, Robert Church, and Johnnie L. Cochran and
a history of rap music. She has also written a children's book about the
life of James Oglethorpe.